MW01046751

Vincent Santelmo

700 E. State Street ▪ Iola, WI 54990-0001
Telephone: 715-445-2214

Library of Congress Catalog Number:
ISBN: 0-87341-301-6
Printed in the United States of America

Dedicated With Love

To my Mom and Dad.
To my generation, the children of the sixties.
To my family and friends.
To my significant other, Mindy.
To my fantastic plastic friend, GI Joe.

Contents

Foreword

In 1964, a new era in American culture began. It was the year that GI Joe was born.

In the thirty years between then and now, GI Joe has traveled around the globe and lived thousands of adventures. He has come to symbolize a rite of passage for all boys, and at the same time represent the ultimate hero. He is a hero the world has counted on and trusted in for over three decades. He is every man, a champion whose only powers are his guts, his heart, and his American spirit.

This thirty-year history has been compiled painstakingly by Vincent Santelmo, Krause Publications, and all of us at Hasbro. It is the only book of its kind and the official history of GI Joe.

This wonderful book represents a chronicle of the last thirty years and a celebration of the next 30! It comes to you from people who not only love GI Joe, but believe in the child in all of us and the backyard adventures we all still dream of.

Vincent D'Alleva
GI Joe Director
Hasbro, Inc.

Preface

My fascination with GI Joe began the day I got my first Action Soldier as a Christmas present in 1964. When GI Joe entered my life that year, I started collecting. I even joined the GI Joe Club.

My mom and dad bought me a lot of GI Joes, and my family helped out by giving me GI Joe equipment and accessories for my birthday, Christmas, and other special occasions. I built a great collection of official equipment, piece by piece.

During my childhood, I had many different dolls and toys, but GI Joe was my favorite.

—Vince Santelmo

In Memory of...

my Aunt Phil, who smuggled in my first GI Joe Action Soldier as a Christmas present in 1964. I wish Aunt Phil could see me now.

To my Uncle Vinny. In World War II, Uncle Vinny was in charge of an M-51 machine gun crew that fought in the Battle of the Bulge. Uncle Vinny *was* GI Joe!

To my grandparents, Vincent and Mary Santelmo, and Joseph and Elizabeth Guida.

And to Merrill and Stephen Hassenfeld, who loved GI Joe more than anyone else.

Acknowledgments

During the creation of this book I required some assistance along the way. I sincerely thank all my friends for their positive show of support, enthusiasm and especially for their contributions to this, my second GI Joe project. This book would not have been as informative as it is without the help of these people. And to all the people not listed, who have in some way given of their time, knowledge and support. I thank you all for your best wishes for the success of this book.

To the people (past and present) at Hasbro

I would like to thank CEO Alan Hassenfeld and the Hasbro company for exclusive permission to use their GI Joe trademark, for providing me with the materials that I needed to successfully complete the job, and especially for giving their blessing to both my volumes on GI Joe. I thank the following group of company employees for their personal interest and help:

Barry Alperin
Beth Buvarsky
Greg Berndtson
Kirk Bozigian
Wayne Charness
Sandy Cabral
Vinnie D'Alleva
Dave DesForges
Kurt Groen
Norm Jacques
Bill Lansing
Dave LeBlanc
Don Levine
Tom McCarthy
Laura Millhollin
Jerry Pilkington
Bob Prupis
Ron Rudat
Gary Serby

To friends and collectors

I sincerely thank my friend, Peter Ruisi, for all of the help that he gave me regarding the entire 3¾ inch GI Joe series. Peter's extensive knowledge of the 1980s and 1990s lines, combined with the figures from his private collection he allowed me to photograph, really added spice to both my volumes on GI JOE. His dedication as a collector has been much appreciated.

Many thanks also go to my collecting buddy Roddy Garcia, whom I've known since the day in 1984 I began my interest in GI Joe. Over the years, as we have grown in the hobby, his passion for GI Joe has remained a positive source of inspiration. I appreciate his sincere interest in my work.

Thanks to Lenny Lee of *Action Figure News and Toy Review* for his help with the *Star Wars* figures and information.

Thanks to Michael O'Neil for his help in identifying the correct names for the 1980s series figures.

I also would like to thank collectors Joe Desris and Hal Fowler for their special contributions.

And many thanks to Sunny Fine (Sunshine Productions) for her dedicated time, and the portraits she photographed of both me and my GI Joe collection.

To the people at Krause Publications

I extend my sincere apreciation and thanks to the publishers of both my books, *The Complete Encyclopedia to GI Joe* and *The Official 30th Anniversary Salute to GI Joe.* Many people at the company were involved personally in making these books become a reality: Greg Smith, Publisher; Pat Klug, Book Division Manager; Mary Seiber and Nathan Unseth, my editors.

To Steven Leszczysnski

The attorney who helped make it all come together.

Introduction

GI Joe action figure collecting has been one of America's most popular hobbies, ever since the movable soldier made his debut back in 1964. Hasbro's GI Joe has been the world's largest ongoing series of modern "action figures," and collecting of GI Joe and his "official" equipment is as popular today as when he was introduced.

For many reasons men and women, young and old, are intrigued by this renowned, collectible toy. I collect GI Joe because I had him as a child during the 1960s and 1970s. Thousands of other people collect GI Joe for the same reason, while others may collect him because they like military toys, or because they appreciate all collectible action figures.

Original GI Joe figures and sets were produced by the millions, and a vast selection can be found today, many still in their original boxes. Many of the first GI Joe figures and sets are still in the possession of their original owners. Nonetheless, collectors may find GI Joes and equipment for trade or sale (at affordable prices) in doll and toy collector magazines and shows, at flea markets and bazaars, even at garage sales.

These popular action-adventure figures are currently being produced in both the "standard" 3¾ inch and "classic" 12-inch size. The Hasbro Company, GI Joe's creator, continues to design and manufacture dozens of new and exciting GI Joe sets annually. As with the early products, the new items from the 1990s are highly collectible also.

Depending on rarity and condition, first generation GI Joe sets from the 1960s-1970s series command prices ranging from under $50 to over $2,500. Their counterpart second generation sets from the 1980s-1990s series fetch prices from under $10 to over $250 for certain sets.

In recognition of GI Joe's great popularity, this book commemorates his three decades on the toy scene. That is why it is titled, *The Official 30th Anniversary Salute to GI Joe*. As the second GI Joe reference book officially endorsed by Hasbro, its purpose is not only to celebrate, but to inform as well. A well-informed collector is a confident collector.

This book recounts the years of GI Joe, from the wooden mannequin that inspired artists, to the first socially acceptable "doll" for boys—known as an action figure. It provides an easy to read, profusely illustrated chronicle of the evolution of a toy—and its temporary demise during the late 1970s.

This book also introduces some of the interesting people, past and present, who have had a vital part in creating and producing GI Joe.

If you are not yet a GI Joe enthusiast/collector, I hope this book will help to make you one. There is a large network of collectors and dealers around the world actively buying, selling and trading GI Joes. Get involved, and discover the magic world of GI Joe!

—Vincent Santelmo

This Book Covers Each Set From The Following Series:

1964-1969

Action Soldier
Action Sailor
Action Marine
Action Pilot
Action Soldiers Of The World
GI Nurse—Action Girl
The Adventures Of GI Joe

1970-1978

The GI Joe Adventure Team
The GI Joe Adventure Team with Kung-Fu Grip
The GI Joe Adventure Team with Life-Like Body
Super Joe—Super Adventure Team

1982-1989

GI Joe:
Slaughters Marauders
Battleforce 2000
Tiger Force
Night Force
Sky Patrol
Cobra:
Iron Grenadiers
Python Patrol
Dreadnoks

1990-1993

GI Joe
Cobra
GI Joe and Cobra:
Sonic Fighters
Super Sonic Fighters
Eco Warriors
Talking Battle Commanders
Ninja Force
Drug Elimination Force
Evil Headhunters
Battle Corps
Mega Marines
Mega Monsters
Capcom Street Fighter II
Star Brigade
Hall Of Fame:
GI Joe
Cobra
Capcom Street Fighter II

1994

GI Joe
Cobra
GI Joe and Cobra:
Battle Corps
Shadow Ninja
Star Brigade
Armor Tech
Manimals
Power Fighters
Capcom Street Fighter II
Hall Of Fame:
GI Joe
Cobra
Capcom Street Fighter II
30th Salute

For my father who defied the critics, and my brother who helped build the dream, let me thank you for helping to immortalize GI Joe. As we enter 1994 and GI Joe's birthday, I toast both you and my friend "Joe."

Alan Hassenfeld, CEO
Hasbro, Inc.*

*From a letter written to the author.

CHAPTER ONE

The Birth of GI Joe®

It all started with an idea. In March 1962, independent toy designer Stanley Weston approached Don Levine, Hasbro's creative director of product development, and offered the company a new and unusual concept. Weston thought Levine's company could make a fortune by selling a line of children's toys based on his up-and-coming show, *The Lieutenant*, a TV series scheduled to air that fall.

The show starred Gary Lockwood as

BELOW: GI Joe: One of the most successful toys ever created.

RIGHT:
The cute appearance of Hasbro's early 60s logo belies the "macho" image of the company's new soldier toy.

ABOVE:
The concept of a soldier figure issued from the TV show, *The Lieutenant,* whose lead character was a Marine.

Lieutenant Bill Rice, a soft-core United States Marine. At the time, Weston was selling merchandising rights to this show, so he suggested the idea for a boy's movable soldier figure, much like Mattel's Barbie, to be based on his show's title character. And, like Barbie, the figure could be dressed in different attire.

Weston had conceived the idea after noticing that boys secretly were playing with Mattel dolls. He therefore thought a combat action figure for boys might succeed in toy stores. Levine liked Weston's idea and immediately began the design.

Levine became fascinated with the idea of creating a toy figure based on Lieutenant Bill Rice. For inspiration, Weston showed Levine video clips from *The Lieutenant* and parts of the script. After sitting through the show's pilot episode, however, Levine discarded the idea of a tie-in. He had two reasons: first, the series really was for adults, and second, he did not want to risk tying a product to a show that might easily be cancelled.

One cold February day in 1963, while trying to come up with ideas, Levine happened to look into the display window of an art supply store. There it was, standing alone on a top shelf: a sculptor's wooden mannequin. This jointed model, used by art students, could be bent on ball joints and hinges.

Suddenly the idea came to him—a Barbie-sized boy's soldier with movable parts. Levine would make a fully articulated military action figure just like that mannequin, but constructed of plastic.

"Those models were what really did it for me," said Levine, who eventually left the company in 1972 to form his own toy-design firm. "I bought a dozen of 'em and we dressed them up in military uniforms so our engineers and the plastic people could see how that thing could bend. We felt that in order to be successful, the figure had to be very flexible. He wasn't like Barbie—all she ever had to do was sit in her car."

Levine was sure that little boys would enjoy posing the doll in as many different positions as they could. Thus the brilliant idea for the first "movable action figure" was born.

Levine also believed that real service

uniforms and equipment should be scaled to fit the new toy. This was the idea behind open-end merchandising, a concept that concentrates on accessories—a concept that was credited for the extreme success of Mattel's Barbie doll series. Levine then met with Merrill Hassenfeld, Hasbro's president, and presented Weston's idea.

Hassenfeld was delighted with the entire concept and ultimately authorized its purchase. Weston received a lump sum payment of $100,000 for the original idea—but gave up a royalty offer that would have awarded him millions.

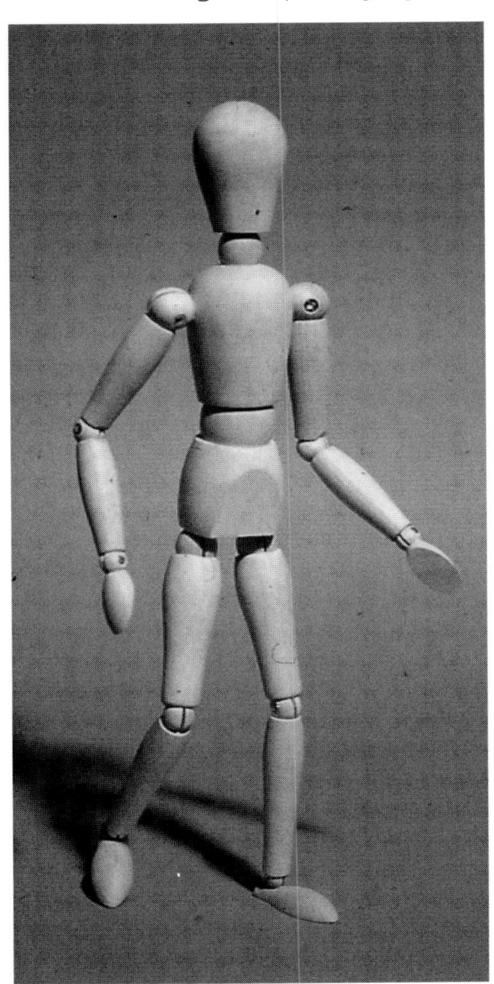

LEFT: The inspiration for the movable "action figure": an artist's multi-jointed mannequin.

Despite Hassenfeld's consent and Levine's enthusiasm, not everyone at Hasbro was convinced, but Levine was persuasive. He recalls, "Everyone kept telling us, You guys are crazy—a boy will never play with a *doll!*" So I got up in front of a sales meeting that first year and said, "Hey, fellas, don't ever sell this as a doll. It's a *movable soldier*. And besides, when the country's not at war, military toys do very well—the graph goes way up."

Once the toy concept had been acquired, Hassenfeld authorized Levine to spend some $30,000 making up samples so he could flesh out the concept. To get started, Levine surrounded himself with real Army helmets, uniforms, and an assortment of weaponry, all for inspiration.

After the concept was clarified, mold-makers Samuel Speers and Hugh O'Connor engineered the toy. This included devising a way for the figure to stand on its own (like the wooden mannequin) in many different positions, while holding weapons or equipment.

It was Don Levine who conceived the manly battle scar that snaked down the right cheek of the figure's face. Levine rationalized, "There was no other way to trademark the human body." In addition, the original figure also had a thumbnail on the wrong side of its thumb (at first a simple manufacturing defect), which eventually became another protective measure against patent infringement.

Drawings submitted by Hasbro for its application to patent GI Joe.

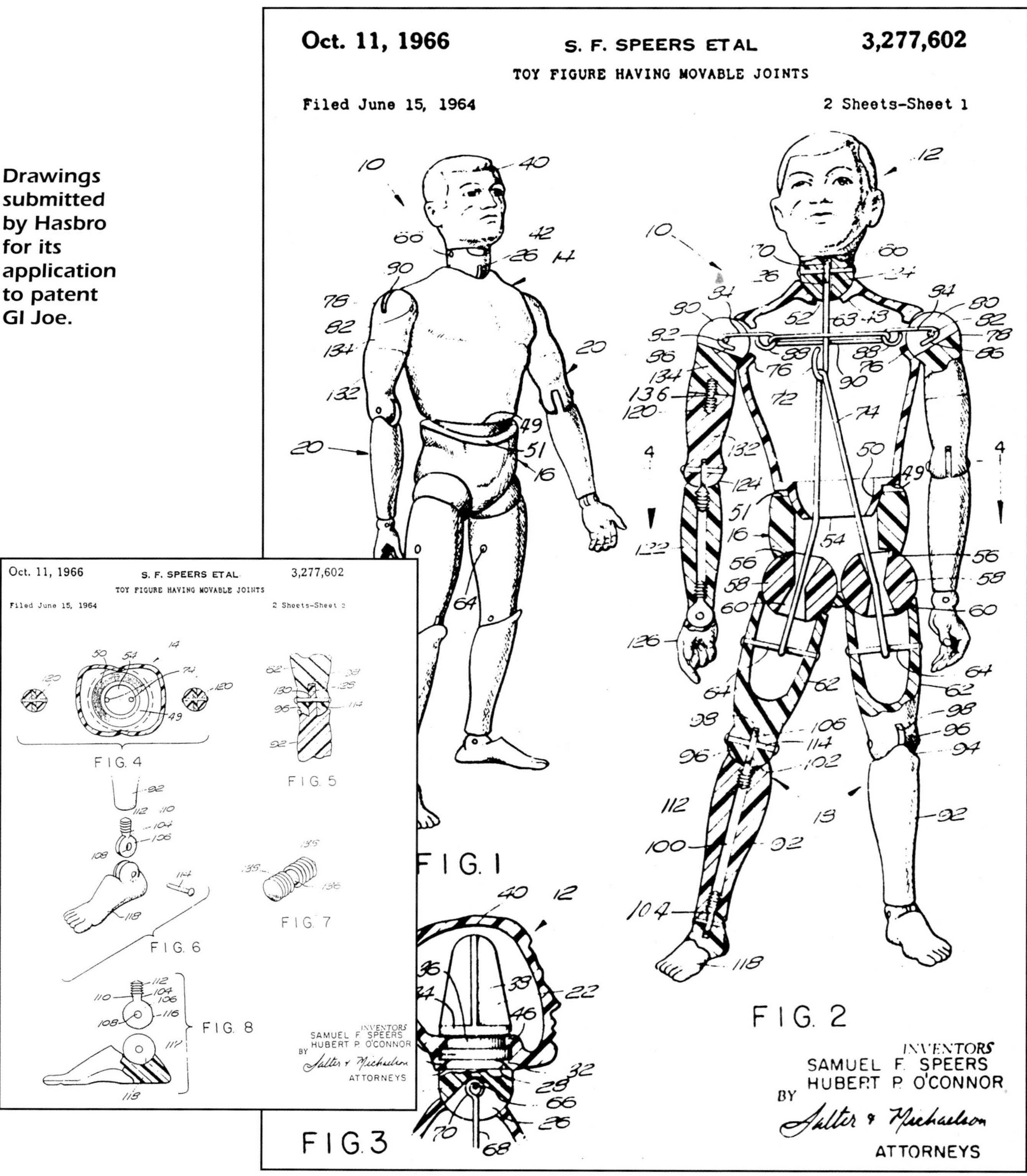

The figure stood at 11½ inches (29 centimeters, or ⅙th scale) because Barbie was that tall. GI Joe, therefore, would be 5 feet, 9 inches tall if he were a real person. Hassenfeld's associate, Walter Hansen, fashioned the sturdy, husky body, while artist Phil Kraczkowski sculpted the head. (Although a publicity campaign by Hasbro's PR department asserted the figure's face was based on a composite of twenty-six Congressional Medal of Honor recipients, the claim is untrue.)

The toy took shape through scores of drawings and studies on the drafting table, after which diagrams were sent to engineering to determine whether the parts could be molded properly. After that, prototypes were sculpted in the model shop, then submitted for safety review and approval. Once approved they went directly into production.

The goal was to make an inexpensive toy that was relatively simple and economical to manufacture, lightweight yet durable, and safe for

LEFT: GI Joe revealing his trademark scar.

children to play with. When the toy came off of the assembly line later that year, it was fully articulated. Brilliantly engineered, featuring twenty-one moveable parts, each part moved separately to duplicate every conceivable human position. The figure also had either black, blonde, brown or red molded hair, and blue or brown painted eyes.

The figure's head, fabricated in both Hong Kong and Japan, was made of poly-vinyl chloride (PVC). The body was manufactured in the United States of a high-impact styrene plastic, its pieces joined with ball joints, rivets and connector studs. The ball joints were used where the arms and legs met the body and also at the neck, elbows, wrists, knees and ankles. Durable elastic bands with metal hooks secured the parts together. Interestingly, the body portions of GI Joe were stored without heads, making inventory more flexible. As orders demanded, the desired heads would be placed on the figures.

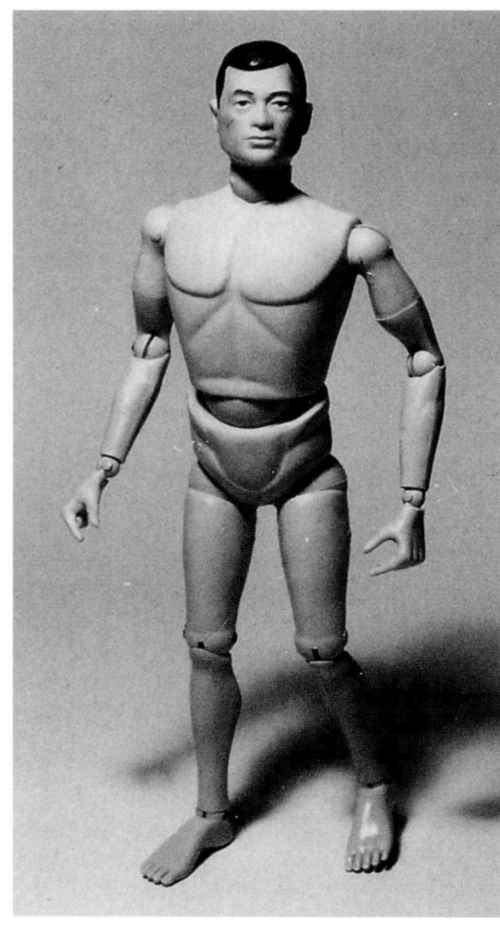

RIGHT: The twenty-one moving parts of GI Joe.

As the unprecedented toy approached completion, its makers still had not settled an important issue: which branch of the military the figure would represent. Hassenfeld suggested issuing an Army soldier one year, closely followed by figures representing the Marines, Navy and Air Force during the three years following, but Levine called that approach "ridiculous." He successfully argued that if the company did not market all four services at once, "Competitors would invade our left and right flank and come up with another figure." (The actual idea for a toy cannot be copyrighted, so a successful new product can be imitated easily.) Hassenfeld conceded.

After overcoming that problem, Levine was faced with another: the figure still lacked a distinctive name. Fred Bruns, Hassenfeld's New York advertising agency, was uninspired by the names Levine had given to the figures, such as Salty the Sailor, Ace the Pilot, and Rocky the Marine.

"They told me that it was like shooting buckshot to use that many names," Levine explained. "They said, 'You guys need a target and one direct hit. " The Bruns agency insisted that the action figure carry only one complete name, but Levine sought fruitlessly for the perfect name.

Levine tried in vain until one evening when he switched on the television set and saw a 1945 war movie, *The Story of GI Joe*, starring Robert Mitchum and Burgess Meredith (as war correspondent Ernie Pyle). There it was, the most readily recognizable military name: *GI Joe*—Government Issue Joe. It was the proud symbol of the American fighting man, taken from one of the best World War II movies ever produced. The name was perfect.

ABOVE: Hasbro's initial GI Joe trademark design.

Hasbro's legal department moved into action and found the "GI Joe" trademark was unclaimed for the toy industry. "It was as if the gods were looking down on us," Levine fondly recalled. So the new product was christened GI Joe.

After consulting military manuals to ensure accuracy, Hasbro designers produced almost every uniform and equipment set for the four branches of service: Army, Navy, Marines and Air Force. Representing each branch would be an Action Soldier, Action Sailor, Action Marine, and Action Pilot. Each GI Joe would come wearing basic military fatigues, including hat, dog tag, jump boots, unit patches, and insignia chevrons, with a field training manual and other exciting extras.

The skills for sewing the miniature uniforms could be found only in the

LEFT: Without the almost mythical name of, GI Joe, this Action Sailor, might have faced life as Salty the Sailor.

Orient, so Levine and GI Joe (with Bill Pressman, a vice president assigned by Hassenfeld to oversee the operation) traveled to Hong Kong and Tokyo, searching for the needed talent. They finally lined up two firms, one in each city, that could do the job. Eventually a sample line was received from overseas. Hassenfeld deemed it "magnificent." Now GI Joe truly was complete, though he still had to face a child—but first, the retailers.

RIGHT: The intricate detail of GI Joe's face and uniform—right down to the military dog tag.

LEFT:
With the help of a film and this comic book, the name GI Joe had become synonymous with military masculinity.

CHAPTER TWO

GI Joe® in the 1960s

"Fighting man from head to toe / On the land, on the sea, in the air."

1964

In January 1964, Hassenfeld brought ten major toy buyers from around the world to New York City to view the line. Hassenfeld said, "If they had turned it down, we would have dropped the project." Actually, the voting was even, but this was encouraging enough for Hassenfeld to enter GI Joe in the annual American International Toy Fair in New York the following month.

GI Joe, Action Soldier.

The problem now was to overcome the trade's objection to a "doll" for boys. Working with his advertising agency, Hassenfeld invested $25,000 to produce a sales film designed to portray GI Joe as a virile fighting man rather than a doll. To maintain secrecy until the last minute, the representatives were shown the film only one day before the toy fair opened.

Throughout the fair, the GI Joe sales film was shown to groups of buyers from all over the world who jammed the showrooms. The film, in the opinion of ad agency president Fredrick Bruns, "did a remarkable selling job. It succeeded in making GI Joe a soldier, which had to be accomplished to attract the trade."

Despite the film's effectiveness,

many buyers still viewed GI Joe skeptically, thinking that a male doll would not appeal to boys. Now Levine had good reason to worry. He had spent over a year developing this toy for what was obviously a highly speculative market. Boys had been playing with little army men for years, but GI Joe was not little. And neither was Hasbro's investment little—more than $2 million.

The buyers purchased only a small amount of merchandise. Then GI Joe was put in New York area stores to test sales. Beginning August 1, 1964, Larry O'Daly, head of advertising and sales promotion, began running one spot a day on one New York television sta-

GI Joe, Action Sailor.

GI Joe, Action Marine.

tion. GI Joe became a hit and sold out in New York within one week.

GI Joe then moved into selected stores across the country and from August 15 to September 15 was pushed through just one spot a week on the NBC television network. Before long, GI Joe had sold out all over, and the nation's toy stores began looking like little military surplus stores. In fact, GI Joe soon was a common item in many kinds of retail outlets, including small supermarkets, pharmacies, stationery stores, and large department stores.

Fortunately for Hassenfeld, millions of kids were watching TV when the company aired its memorable GI Joe commercials later that year. The jingle, sung to the tune of "The Caissons Go Rolling Along," proclaimed, "GI Joe, GI Joe, / Fighting man from head to toe, / On the land, on the sea, in the air." While the narrator announced that GI Joe could "...do anything that a soldier does in bivouac and in battle."

In the commercials, dioramas of GI Joes from all four branches of service, showed the soldier in every conceivable military position imaginable—crouching in a foxhole, storming a beach, throwing a hand grenade, or firing a machine gun. Hundreds of authentic pieces of equipment, including everything from rifles and machine

GI Joe, Action Pilot.

guns to bayonets and full field equipment, made it possible for a boy to build complete bivouac sets and battle scenes. Hasbro's GI Joe ad won an award for best in television commercials. This was just the beginning of GI Joe TV commercials to be seen each year, highlighting the new sets released that year.

Action figures were priced at a suggested retail of $4 each, with uniforms and equipment sets ranging in price from $1 to $5. These items included every kind of gear from land combat to air survival, authentic down to the minutest detail. With these sets a boy could turn any GI Joe into almost any kind of real-life serviceman.

By year's end, four basic figures, six uniforms, and sixty-three equipment sets (in which parts of uniforms were available on individual cards) were available, distributed among GI Joe's four branches of service.

GI Joe's success rested on the same accessory concept that had made Mattel's Barbie so successful, the concept

On the battle field and in the toy store, GI Joe proved to be a formidable foe.

GI Joe, the full-dress Marine.

known in the toy industry as the "razor/razor blade phenomenon." As Levine explained, "You buy the razor, then you've got to buy a lot of blades." In time, after the series had proven itself, the GI Joe name would represent not only the action figures, but the entire product line.

Even though American parents said that they would not buy their sons "dolls," Hasbro persistence paid off. In GI Joe's first year alone, the company raked in $16.9 million, reflecting an estimated sale of two million action figures. As the first male fig-

RIGHT: GI Joe demonstrating the Navy Attack set.

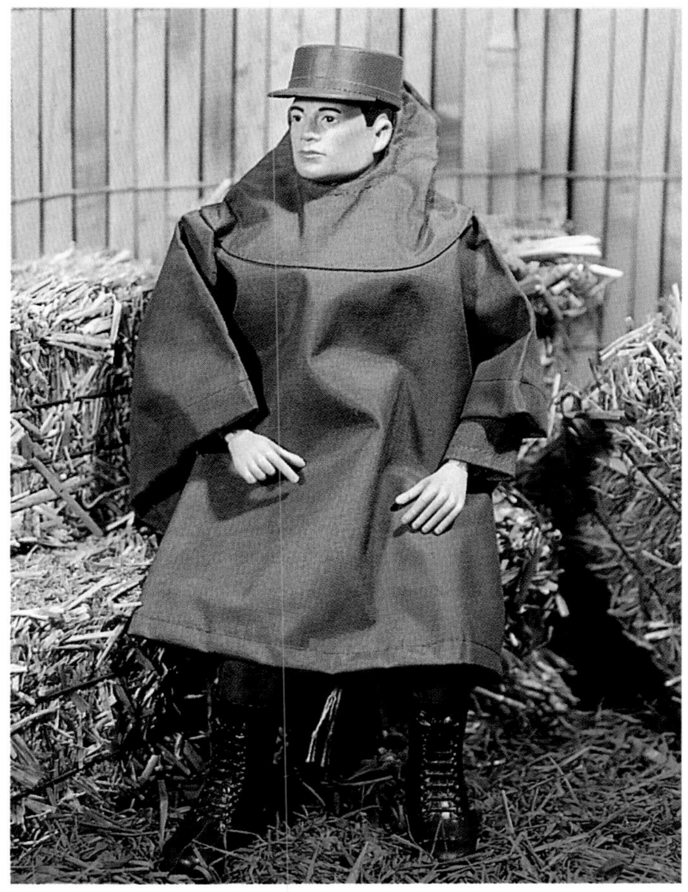

tary hardware, eventually found its way into more than ten million homes nationwide. This proliferation was enough to rank GI Joe as the best-selling single toy among five- to twelve-year-olds. And thanks to this enormous success, Don Levine was promoted to vice president.

At the time, Hasbro was one of the country's five largest toy producers, the other four being General Mills, Mattel, Ideal and Topper Toys, all of which had extensive product lines. About seventy percent of Hasbro's business came from the GI Joe series, so Hasbro set up a separate division to handle the huge number of orders. "The item has become," said Hassenfeld, "a concept—

ure with realistic military equipment, the rough and ready plastic combatant, along with his wide range of mili-

LEFT:
GI Joe was ready for anything, including wet weather, in this poncho.

BELOW:
GI Joe could even have a cot on which to rest!

Thousands have already sent in their names

"JOIN THE G.I. JOE® CLUB!"

G.I. JOE SAYS: SEND IN YOUR NAME TODAY!

Hasbro's brochure promoting the new GI Joe Club.

more than a product."

As further confirmation of the action figure's success, the official GI Joe Club started in December 1964 and soon had enlisted over 150,000 boys and girls, with thousands joining each week. Membership cost only fifty cents, and each recruit received five items: (1) a replica plastic dog tag with a blank area for writing the owner's name, rank and serial number; (2) an iron-on transfer for a t-shirt; (3) a certificate to frame and display; (4) a wallet-sized identification card; and (5) a copy of the GI Joe catalog.

The advertising budget (mostly for TV) for GI Joe was more than $2.5 million. Naturally, other companies tried to copy GI Joe in some way, but Hasbro was secure against any real competition. The company's legal department had long since secured exclusive trademark rights to GI Joe, for everything but movies, in 36 countries. Already about sixty companies had requested use of the name for a variety of products, but Hassenfeld had licensed only a few.

One licensee was the Western

RIGHT: GI Joe equipment manuals, for the American and the Japanese markets.

Publishing Company which issued GI Joe coloring and story books, and another was DC Comics (known as National Periodical Publications until 1976). Late in 1964, DC printed the first GI Joe comic book (since the discontinuation of the original GI Joe comics by Ziff-Davis in 1956). For only twelve cents a GI Joe fan could read action-packed accounts of the exploits of GI Joe in different phases of military service, whether the Army, Navy, Marines or Air Force. (The characters portrayed in these comics were not at all related to Hasbro's GI Joe.)

1965

In the second year, Hasbro's sales

The first black Action Soldier.

of GI Joe more than doubled, grossing $36.5 million. An important factor that increased GI Joe's popularity in 1965 was the introduction of the first black Action Soldier, sold initially in major northern cities.

Another first, a GI Joe Action Soldier combat gift set was sold exclusively at Sears, Roebuck department stores. This set included the basic GI Joe soldier with an assortment of realistic weapons and equipment. This was the first

GI Joe's first vehicle: the authentic Combat Jeep.

GI Joe as a deep-sea diver.

of many different exclusive combination sets available from Sears, Roebuck, J.C. Penney, and Montgomery Ward department stores.

Another reason for GI Joe's overwhelming popularity was the introduction of the jeep combat set, the first vehicle specially scaled to fit GI Joe, designed particularly for the Action Soldier and Marine. This realistic set included the same khaki green four-wheel drive vehicle that more than half of the world's armies used. The vehicle even had working features, such as a battery-operated searchlight which could be used to send signals in Morse code, and a spring-activated recoilless rifle that fired miniature rocket shells. This set sold for $15.

In 1965 two new figure sets, one vehicle, two uniform sets, and eight equipment packages were introduced for GI Joe's four branches of service. The Action Sailor's Deep Sea Diver outfit was the first such set with working features. It enabled kids to submerge GI Joe in water,complete with bubbles rising to the surface. By now there were almost 80 different GI Joe sets, some priced as low as $1.

This year many related products were made available, some manufactured by Hasbro, while others were licensed to companies including Whitman, Watkins and Strathmore, Western Publishing, and Sawyers/GAF. Throughout the 1960s and into the 1970s, these companies produced items such as View-Master picture reels, playing cards, color-forms sets, an inflatable bop-bag punching toy, and a scuba diver pool toy, as well as pinball games, jigsaw puzzles, and Sticker Fun coloring and story books. There was even a GI Joe Activity Box containing punch-out soldiers, and the very popular GI Joe Etch-A-Sketch drawing set from Ohio Art.

For Toy Fair of 1965, Hasbro fea-

GI Joe as a member of the Ski Patrol.

tured a massive GI Joe exhibit in the company showroom in Manhattan. The realistic battle scene, measuring 18 feet by 8 feet, featured almost sixty GI Joe characters from all four branches of service, dressed in battle gear and attacking an enemy position. This diorama remained on display in New York for a few weeks, then moved to a military post in New York Harbor. Soon after, it was relocated to the Gimbels department store. There it became one of the biggest attractions in New York's toy world. Thousands of little boys flocked to the exhibit to see what could be done with GI Joe and his equipment.

By this time Hasbro carried about 300 toys, including the popular Mr. Potato Head®, but the GI Joe line was responsible for the company's surge in revenue. Trade sources estimated that GI Joe had climbed up to about fifth in the toy

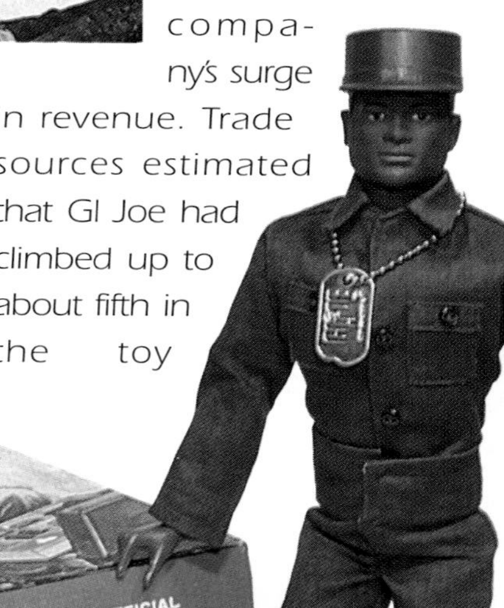

The popular GI Joe footlocker, still in its packaging.

The GI Joe foot-locker and its contents.

field, and the toy was expected to move higher in the next year.

During 1965 the first international license for GI Joe was granted to Palitoy, a British firm. This was the first of many overseas product licenses Hasbro has successfully negotiated. The British line was named Action Man. Each figure was made from the original GI Joe molds, and some equipment pieces were the same as the original. However, Palitoy's uniform and vehicle sets, in addition to offering a broader selection, were considered (by collectors) more realistic in many ways than Hasbro's GI Joe.

The GI Joe Club added a sixth membership extra: a copy of the monthly newsletter, *Command Post News*. The *News*, about real GI Joes in battle. The *News* also included articles on military history, tactics and jar-

The British version of GI Joe: Action Man from Palitoy.

gon, and patriotic messages from Colonel Pat Lawrence, commanding officer at GI Joe Club headquarters. *Command Post News* also kept members informed of all of new GI Joe equipment. The club was promoted through stuffers packaged with each action figure and set, through comic book coupons, through recruiting posters in toy stores, and through television commercials.

1966

As American toy makers increased production of Vietnam combat toys, to reassert its leadership Hasbro introduced an entirely new combat package featuring the Special Forces Green Beret figure and equipment set. Modeled after the legendary hero of the Vietnam War, this set included a basic

GI Joe as a member of the elite Special Forces, better known as the Green Beret.

GI Joe goes international, with Action Soldiers of the World.

GI Joe Action Soldier (in assorted hair and eye color) uniformed in a hot weather jungle uniform similar to that worn by John Wayne in the motion picture, *The Green Berets*. The set came with a miniature M-16 rifle, communications set, and other pieces of equipment, at a price of $8.

The Green Beret package was followed closely by the Green Beret Machine Gun Outpost set—a Sears, Roebuck gift exclusive. This Action Soldier package included two GI Joes of the Green Beret, each uniformed in camouflage. They were replete with equipment and weaponry that included a Special Forces camouflaged bazooka that could fire miniature M-20 anti-tank rockets.

Sears carried yet another exclusive item, the Forward Observer set. The package contained the GI Joe figure clad in full combat fatigues, and equipped with command post and Army bivouac equipment and weapons, such as a .30 caliber tripod-mounted machine gun that swiveled. This set sold for $6.98. No new figure sets were made for the GI Joe Sailor, Marine or Pilot.

During this year Hasbro also introduced the GI Joe Combat Series, Action Soldiers of the World. Special features made these models much different from those of previous years. Intended especially for World War II collectors, this set offered six soldiers of foreign countries that fought in World War II: Germany, Japan, Russia, France, Britain, and Australia.

When these soldiers first hit toy stores, the figures actually were the basic GI Joe of earlier years, complete with the battle scar. However, soon after their release, Hasbro replaced the "all-American" look with "foreign" heads designed by Virginia Gardner Perry. Five of the soldiers had the same

LEFT:
A Japanese Imperial soldier.

RIGHT:
A British commando.

LEFT:
A Russian infantryman.

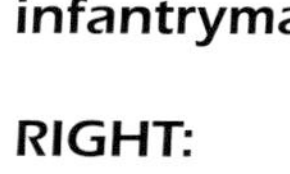

RIGHT:
A German trooper.

LEFT:
An Australian soldier.

RIGHT:
A French resistance fighter.

Officer set; the Air Force Crash Crew Fire Fighter set; the Army Jungle Fighter accessories set; the Navy Sea Rescue set; the Marine Demolotion set(with a battery-powered red detection light that glowed when the unit scanned a land mine).

Two vehicle sets were added to the line, the first being the Action Sailor Frogman and Sea Sled set, which included a perfectly-detailed, battery-powered orange aqua sled that could dive, run submerged, and surface. The set's GI Joe Sailor wore an orange wet suit with miniature

LEFT: The *GI Joe Counter-Intelligence Manual* for the Soldiers of the World series.

face sharply-sculpted Nordic head, available in assorted hair and eye colors. The Japanese figure, of course, had definite Asian features. Each of the Soldiers of the World could be purchased in a basic package for $5. Additional equipment was available on a separate card, priced at $2.79. Hasbro also offered fully-equipped deluxe sets for $8.

This year many new uniforms and equipment packages were introduced for GI Joe, including the Army Special Forces set; the Navy Landing Signal

The finely-detailed Landing Signal set.

face mask, oxygen tanks, and swim fins. The set retailed for about $14. (For a few dollars more, Sears offered the set with an exclusive underwater cave and marker buoy.)

The second GI Joe vehicle of 1966 was the Action Pilot Space Capsule set. The one-man craft, a replica of the spaceship in which astronaut John Glenn orbited the earth, came with a space suit made from the same silver metallic fabric as the suits worn by NASA astronauts. Featuring a helmet with working visor, communications plug-in, metallic gloves, and boots, it sold for $7.99. This set also included a 45-rpm sound effects record of the first American orbital space flight. Again, Sears offered an exclusive version that added an inflatable flotation collar, life raft, and oar, for $2 more.

Although the extensive GI Joe product line was voted number one among children in 1966, market surveys revealed that kids' interests were turning to adventure themes. After learning this, company president Merrill Hassenfeld said that GI Joe needed "repositioning," and that "it was important that parents view him as more than just a military figure."

This change in the market induced rival toy companies to market their own lines of action figures as alternatives to Hasbro's military GI Joe. Mattel created Captain Laser and Major Matt Mason. Ideal offered Captain Action, complemented by super-pal Action Boy and enemy Doctor

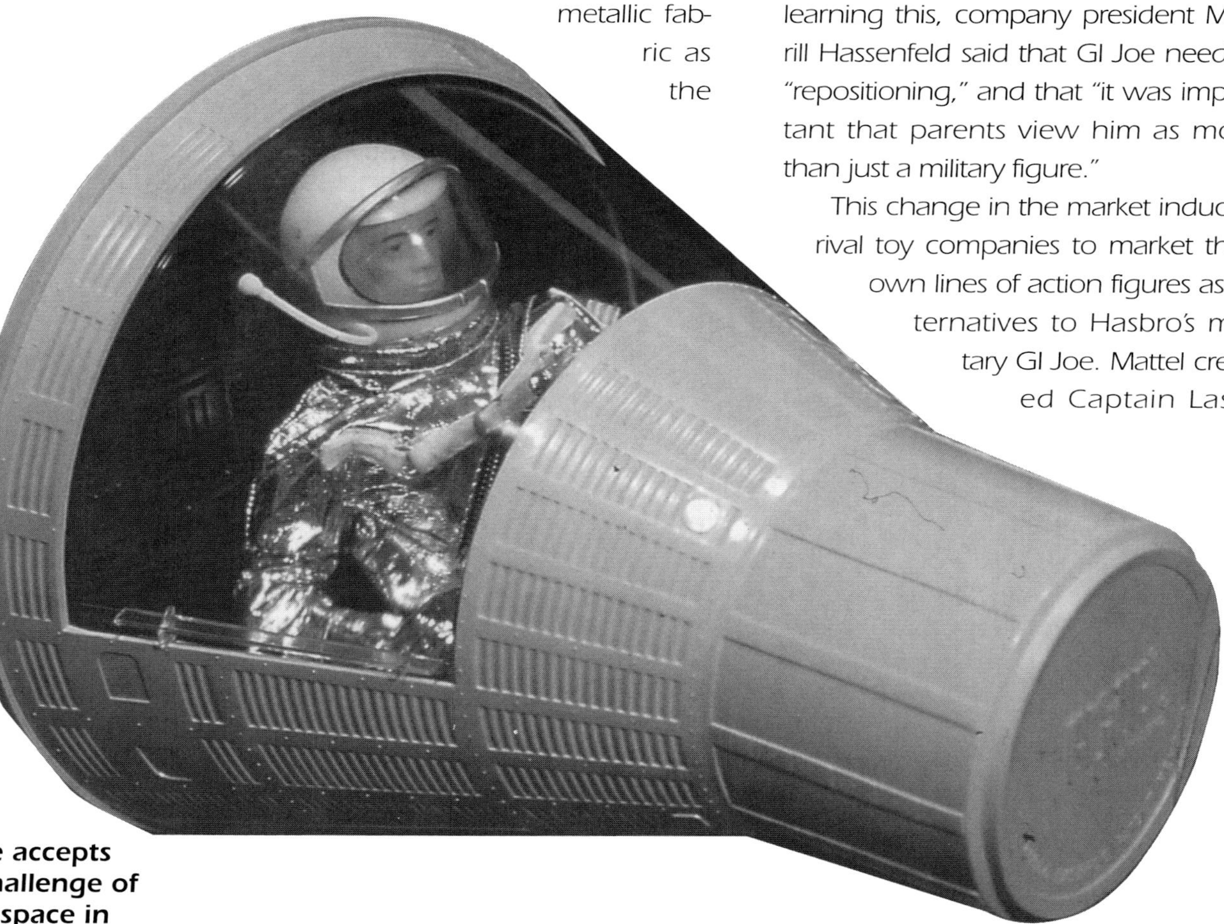

GI Joe accepts the challenge of outer space in his space capsule.

The Gilbert combat watch was one of many licensed GI Joe products.

Evil. Gilbert produced the Man From UNCLE series and the 007 series, as well as Moon McDare and his Space Mutt. Marx featured Stony Stonewall Smith, and the Best of the West series featuring Johnny and Jane West.

Despite such imitation, GI Joe routed all rivals. And to insure his dominance, newly designed versions of the toy were expected to be released during the next year.

In addition to the sets made for GI Joe, child-sized items were offered exclusively through the GI Joe Fan Club. Now kids could look and act like their favorite toy soldier. Some of these popular items were a sleeping bag set, web gun belt, jungle canteen set, and an underwater frogman set.

Other GI Joe promotional items included toy shaving kits, pencil cases, a combat medic doctor's kit, shoe shine boxes, a disguise wig and glasses set, lunch boxes complete with vacuum bottle, and a waterproof poncho, each ranging in price from $2.75 to $4.50. Under license, the Gilbert Company produced a $3.99 GI Joe wristwatch that featured both a compass and a Morse code signaling device.

As a further extension of the line, Hasbro introduced the "Let's Go Joe" board game. A second board game, "Capture Hill 79," also joined the line. In this game, secret orders on playing cards appeared when placed under water.

Hasbro used the comic strip characters, Andy and George, to promote the GI Joe Club—which promoted GI Joe products.

To promote its stream of new products, Hasbro, through DC Comics, published *The Adventures of Andy and George in the GI Joe Club*. Each of the ten issues featured the title characters using newly released GI Joes and sets. This strategy, of course, gave kids the incentive to purchase the same figures and equipment that Andy and George had.

1967

Although the people at Hasbro believed GI Joe "still performed a basic function in providing boys with an acceptable form of doll play," the market was demanding a new version of GI Joe. Nonetheless, Hasbro was reluc-

The GI Joe Talking Sailor offered a reason to buy even more GI Joe figures.

talking GI Joe, with a suggested retail price of $7, was unique in the toy industry and was received with great success.

Outside the U.S., Hasbro/Canada produced the Canadian Mountie set, which included a basic GI Joe in an authentic Royal Canadian Mounted Police uniform. This gift set came with an assortment of weapons, mountain climbing gear, and other equipment. The package was sold only at Simpson-Sears of Canada.

Hasbro/Canada also introduced the short-lived Action Joe line, which featured two vehicle/figure sets. Each set contained a finely detailed, plastic vehicle, and a basic GI Joe clad in complete uniform with equipment.

ABOVE: Hasbro/Canada marketed this Royal Canadian Mountie set.

RIGHT: Also unique to Canada were this state trooper motorcyclist and race car driver.

tant to change a product that had been so successful. Change thus came gradually.

This year saw the debut of the talking GI Joe at the annual Toy Fair in New York. As with the original GI Joe, the talking figures represented the four branches of military service, but each figure could issue eight different "combat commands," activated by pulling GI Joe's dog tag to a different length for each command. The

These sets were the State Trooper on a Harley-Davidson with side car, and the Race Car Driver in a grand prix Lotus.

In an attempt to enter the girls' market, Hasbro introduced its first GI Nurse (the only female figure in the current all-male series) for girls aged four to twelve. GI Nurse stood 10½ inches tall, was fully articulated, and featured 18 movable parts. Her rooted hair and eyelashes could be combed. The nurse came with a regulation 1960s uniform, including hospital dress, nylon stockings, shoes, Red Cross cap and arm band, as well as stethoscope, plasma bottle, bandages, splints, crutches, and other items.

To Hasbro's disappointment, girls showed little interest in an army nurse doll (especially when fashion dolls, e.g. Mattel's Barbie, were much more appealing), and boys did not want the GI Nurse in their ranks. According to reports, no more than 15,000 GI Nurse figures were sold that year. (See "The Female 'Joes'" section later in this chapter.)

This year's uniforms for the Army GI Joe ranged from a West Point Cadet set to a Military Police set. The Navy GI Joe was issued uniforms such as the Shore Patrol and the Breeches Buoy. The GI Joe Marine gained uniform sets such as Tank Commander and the popular Jungle Fighter. And the Air Force GI Joe gained an Air Academy Cadet set and an Air/Sea Rescue set.

GI Joe on parade as a West Point Cadet.

GI Joe in full regalia as an Air Cadet.

The extremely popular Desert Patrol Vehicle, which now can command thousands of dollars.

Army equipment for this year ranged from a Combat Rifle/Helmet set to a Combat Demolition set. For the Marine, the assortment included a Communications Field set and a Weapons Rack. Air Force accessories extended from the Scramble Flight Suit to the Mae West Air Vest set. (Nothing new was produced for the Navy.)

The J.C. Penney stores exploited the action figure's success with a selection of unofficial products (manufactured by independent vendors) that were sold alongside Hasbro's GI Joe products. These items included a Tote-A-Tent, Action Foot Locker, Action Headquarters, Carry Case, Carry Locker, Jungle Station Bunkhouse, and Mobile Sentry Tower.

Highlights for this year included more vehicle sets (some with only uniforms, and others complete with a GI

GI Joe and the Crash Crew Fire Truck, ready for action.

Joe). The very popular desert patrol attack jeep, for instance, was inspired by television's popular *Rat Patrol.* The soldier figure came dressed in Australian type uniform, complete with a .45 caliber pistol. His tan desert vehicle featured a turret-mounted .50 caliber machine gun.

Another package, the Action Pilot Crash Crew Fire Truck set, came complete with an authentic fire fighter's heat suit—made from the same silvery metallic material used by crash fire fighters of the U.S. Air Force. The blue truck displayed Air Force insignias, and had a battery-operated siren and red blinking light. Other features were a fireman's ax, a swiveling extension ladder, and a fire hose that could shoot a stream of water more than 10 feet (powered by a hand pump).

During the height of GI Joe's popularity, the Irwin Company began manufacturing GI Joe merchandise under

The new 32-page *Command Post Yearbook* for members of the GI Joe Club.

license from Hasbro. Irwin's line of combat vehicles were available only at Sears. The popular Irwin line consisted of seven tough, armored vehicles, including the Army Helicopter and the Personnel Carrier/Mine Sweeper. Some models were friction-powered for "live action" sound.

In January 1967, *Command Post News* announced an innovative sweepstakes based on the GI Joe game, "Capture Hill 79." A fan had to go to the nearest toy store and pick up a "magic war map," take it home, then place it in water to make a lucky number appear. Even if the number did not match any in the grand prize list on the toy store's display, the holder could send in the card to be eligible for a drawing for 14,001 other prizes—including cash and GI Joe merchandise.

Now in its fourth year, the GI Joe Club offered its members a new benefit. The club catalog had been replaced by a 32-page *Command Post Yearbook*. The Hasbro company boasted that over 400,000 kids had joined the GI Joe Club. Even more significant, in four short years Hasbro's sensational GI Joe had grossed more than $100 million.

1968

This year, a number of GI Joe figures and sets were discontinued while others were added or reissued. A major concept this year was the Adventure Pack. Both the basic and talking GI Joes from the Army, Navy and Marines (but not the Action Pilot) appeared in Adventure Pack sets, each

GI Joe, as a fighter pilot, struggles with his parachute.

The "4 Services in 1 Special" contained uniforms and equipment for all four major service branches.

displaying a battle scene on its box. The sets offered from thirteen to twenty-four pieces of clothing and equipment.

To complement the American services talking figure sets, Hasbro released a talking GI Joe Foreign Soldiers of the World Adventure Pack set. Each set supplied one "no-scar" Joe, with German, Japanese or Russian uniform and equipment. These sets offered over thirty-nine pieces.

A new equipment set produced this year was the Action Soldier Combat set, the only one that provided GI Joe with a full field assortment of weapons and equipment.

Another new uniform/equipment item in 1968 was the GI Joe Adventure Pack "4 Services in 1 Special." This set contained dress parade uniforms and equipment for each service branch.

Four other "4 Services In 1 Special" sets were employed to reissue combinations of twelve to sixteen pieces of gear. Four accessory cards, one for each branch of service, were packaged in each box.

For each branch of service some GI Joe uniform/equipment sets were reissued this year in newly styled pack-

GI Joe's new image.

In addition to action figures and accessories, Hasbro offered several other GI Joe products. These included board games with names such as "Combat Infantry," and "Navy Frogman"; Rub-Ons magic picture transfers; and a target game with a rubber-dart gun.

To help GI Joe fans experience the role of their favorite action soldier, Hasbro introduced sets of kid-size military gear. These Backyard Patrol sets included: ages. The 1967 versions, which had come in windowed boxes, were now issued in boxes bearing a real-life photo and an illustration of the contents.

In a new twist on an old package, Hasbro offered three different GI Joe Foot Locker Adventure Packs. Identical to the green wooden Army foot locker of 1964, the box held fifteen to twenty pieces of military equipment. Issuing the various Adventure Pack sets was one method Hasbro used to phase out the military items, thus making way for

LEFT:
GI Joe, with his Deep Freeze set, appears able to handle anything winter hurls at him.

With flame thrower at hand, this Action Marine is equipped with the Jungle Fighter set.

This Military Police set is perfect to the smallest detail.

Rather than stubbornly dig in against such pressures and risk erosion of sales, Hasbro explored ways of changing GI Joe's military image. Explained Levine, "We decided to soften him, make him more of a James Bond character."

As they strategized such a change, the people at Hasbro wondered if the military-sounding name of GI Joe was part of the problem—but decided the name could not be changed. As Hassenfeld noted, "The buyers would not have bought the new toy without the old name." In the end, GI Joe's image was acceptably redesigned, and a television advertising campaigned was prepared to promote the "new" GI Joe.

mess kit with canteen; pistol and helmet; walkie-talkies; flare gun flashlight; pup tent; field pack and shovel; military police set; and others.

Despite their success, Hasbro and its GI Joe were forced to weather government and consumer reproach. The Federal Trade Commission, Food and Drug Administration, Federal Communications Commission, Consumer Union, and the Parents Group each were attacking the $2.5 billion toy industry. Industry observers also were accusing the industry of deceptive advertising.

Sales of GI Joe had helped increase Hasbro, Inc.'s sales from $25.5 million in 1964 to more than $41 million in 1968. Such encouraging growth was dimmed, however, by the fact that growth had slowed—sales had been projected at $55 million. The following year, therefore, would be crucial to the future of GI Joe.

No longer an Action Sailor, GI Joe the Adventurer is now an Aquanaut.

1969

GI Joe commenced his sixth year with a totally new look. His hard-core military image had changed dramatically to an "Adventurer" concept, accompanied by an aggressive expansion of the GI Joe line.

Using the same basic mannequins, Hasbro reintroduced GI Joe as a member of a crack team of technicians who aided important individuals and governments in adventurous tasks. Instead of an Action Soldier, GI Joe would now assume a wide variety of paramilitary roles, including space explorer and oceanographer.

The company already had tested these new versions of the toy on children to determine which was the most fun in play. The research paid off with strong sales of the new Adventures of GI Joe line. The introductory series offered an Adventurer, a black Adventurer, an Aquanaut, and a talking Astronaut. These Adventurers were advertised as "Brave, strong and tough....Ready to take up man's fight against nature's elements."

Each new GI Joe came in a nondescript uniform, complete with dog tag, boots, a revolver and shoulder holster (not included with talking astronaut).

A large assortment of new vehicles and uniform/equipment sets complemented the new Adventurers. Themes for these sets ranged from aquatic, polar and space exploration, to the capture of wild animals on safari. GI Joe no longer was defending himself with heavy artillery or hand-to-hand combat. Now he was in pursuit of octopi, alligators and sharks. The sets were available in basic, deluxe, and super deluxe versions. Each set was accompanied by a sixteen-page full-color

A "before and after" comparison of GI Joe as Action Soldier and as Land Adventurer.

The Negro Adventurer was the second black GI Joe in the 1960s series. This figure is extremely rare.

comic book that detailed the complete adventure portrayed by that particular figure.

A nostalgic throwback to the original GI Joe was the footlocker. In this case, a personalized foot locker was available for each of the Adventurers. Replete with compartments and a lift-out tray, each footlocker provided an authentic means of storing GI Joe's gear.

The transformation of GI Joe was not confined to toys. GI Joe Club members discovered a significant change in this year's Command Post Yearbook: Thanks to Joe's new image, the word "war" had been replaced by "action adventure." And, of course, the centerfold insert which once showcased Joe's military equipment now displayed the new action adventure line in "The Adventures of GI Joe."

Reincarnated as an Adventurer, the new GI Joe had made a dramatic debut. However, despite expectations to exceed 1968's $6 million profit, Hasbro lost almost $1 million. The loss was attributed to missed deadlines by suppliers in Asia, poor cost control, and a Teamsters strike.

Despite the surging sales of the new GI Joe, the passing of the original Action Soldier was not universally celebrated. As one hard-core GI Joe collector, Roddy Garcia, noted, "1969 marked the end of the golden era of GI Joe."

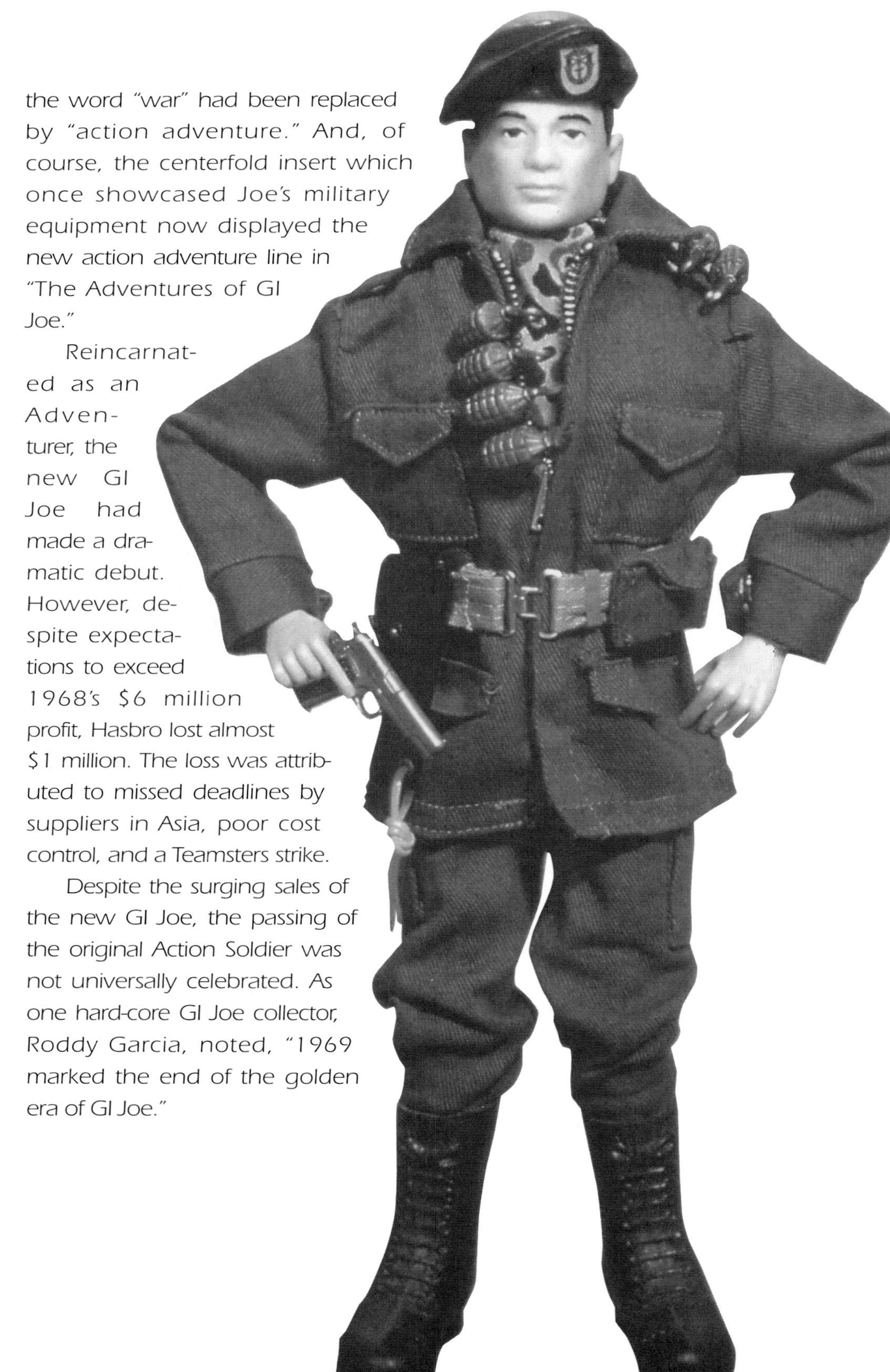

The fighting GI Joe is giving way to a new image.

The Female "Joes"

Hasbro's introduction of a female GI Nurse into the previously all-male GI Joe series was an attempt to extend the line into the girls' market. Because accessory-focused fashion dolls—especially Mattel's Barbie—were flourishing, it seemed wise to gain a share of that market.

Unfortunately, the foray into the girls' market proved to be a flop—for the girls' *and* the boys' market. Girls showed little enthusiasm for a World War II-inspired action doll, preferring the more glamorous fashion dolls they already owned. On the other hand, boys—the core GI Joe market—eschewed the idea of a girls' "doll"—especially if their sisters were playing with it!

In the 1980s, Hasbro again tried to release female figures for the series, with unspectacular results. Collectors have profited, because the value of a female figure skyrockets after it has been discontinued. When the original GI Nurse was released it sold for $8. Today, the same figure "never removed from the box" commands up to $2,500 in the

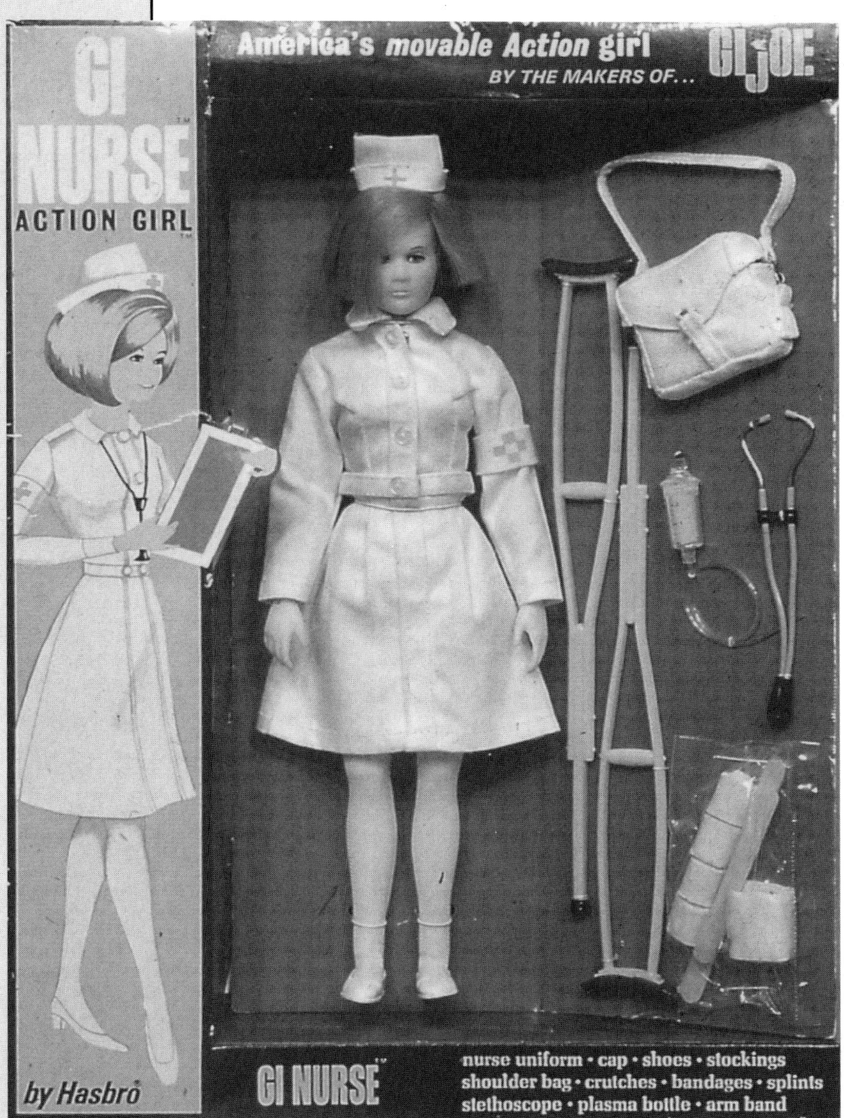

The new GI Nurse, still in its package.

Though adding an interesting element to the GI Joe series, GI Nurse failed to generate much enthusiasm.

volatile GI Joe collectors market. Hasbro, however, isn't in the business of producing collectible toys.

Since the Hall of Fame rocketed to success, collectors have wondered if the most popular females in the standard 3¾ inch series would ever be introduced as characters in the classic 12-inch line. Candidates would be, to name a few, figures such as Scarlett, Lady Jaye, and the Cobra Baroness—the three most popular female figures. Hasbro sources indicate that Hasbro would not consider such a venture without a guaranteed sale of at least 100,000 units.

Commenting on the sale of female figures, Vice-President of Boy's Toys Marketing, Kirk Bozigian, said, "We've done a

number of female Joes, and people forget that the first year's figure line had Scarlett. We followed that up with a driver called Cover Girl and the reason we put her in a vehicle was because Scarlett didn't sell. So, we thought that maybe we could sell a female character if we put her in a vehicle that kids would want—and she didn't sell, but we stayed with it.

"We did the Baroness, Lady Jaye and we did Jinx (she was one of the Ninjas years ago). We recently reintroduced

The most popular female GI Joe figures in years to come: Scarlett, Lady Jaye, and Baroness.

A sketch of a future female action figure.

Scarlett as part of the Ninja Force.

"It's still pretty early to see if she's going to sell or not, but if you look at what goes on in all the other boys' lines, the female figures are the weakest sellers. Now you do them to round out a line, to complete a play scenario, but you can't bank on them being successful. They just aren't. To a collector they're important, but...they're the last thing a five-year-old boy wants."

To date, Hasbro has been reasonably successful in marketing its line of female figures by being careful not to overproduce them. As a matter of fact, the company purposely has made the female figures in limited quantities so they will become more collectible—thus assuring steady sales.

Hasbro's GI Joe division is looking at a female addition to the Hall of Fame. They are not sure who she will be or when she will make her debut—although the Baroness is the favorite of many. As Hasbro's Direct Marketing department works on the idea, the potential of a destined-to-be-valuable female Hall Of Fame character (with guaranteed sales) may be a marketing plus.

Chun-Li, a female figure from the 1993 Streetfighter II series.

CHAPTER THREE

GI Joe® in the 1970s

1970

In an aggressive expansion of the Adventurer theme, this year Hasbro introduced the GI Joe Adventure Team—also known as the A-Team.

Hasbro's magazine ads declared, "These brave Adventurers were designed to relive the adventures of America's most favorite men—dedicated to working together for the good of mankind."

The new version of the basic figure boasted lifelike hair, with some models sporting a beard. GI Joe's hair even was washable. (Palitoy, GI Joe's British licensee, had devised a process by which simulated hair fiber could be sprayed onto the figure's head. At first hair fiber was sprayed right onto the painted hair of existing figures until the inventory was exhausted.)

Through this entire metamorphosis the 1960s Action Soldier became the Man of Action; the black Action Soldier became the Ad-

LEFT: Members of the colorful Adventure Team.

RIGHT:
The shiny suit for the Hidden Missle Discovery set gave this outfit an exotic character.

venturer; the Action Sailor became the Sea Adventurer; the Action Marine became the Land Adventurer; and the Action Pilot became the Air Adventurer.

Thanks to the flocked hair GI Joe now stood almost one foot tall. However, he still bore his battle scar, still had twenty-one movable parts,and still came completely and realistically equipped. Buyers at the New York Toy Fair thought the new GI Joe Adventurer with lifelike hair and beard would be a great seller—and they ordered accordingly.

The new Adventure Team figures were issued in special uniforms (adaptations of earlier styles). Each figure wore a round A-Team medallion that reversed to be a dog tag, adventure boots, and a six-shot revolver with shoulder holster, and each was accompanied by appropriate paperwork.

In addition to the core group of figures, Hasbro continued to launch new GI Joes. The year's introductions included a talking Adventure Team Commander ("the leader of the crack Adventure Team"), a talking astronaut was produced (the same as the 1969 version, but with lifelike hair), and a talking Man of Action (a modified version of the talking Action Soldier from the late 1960s).

By the second half of 1970, sales of GI Joe had

RIGHT:
The Air Adventurer featured a bright orange jumpsuit.

surged strongly upward, indicating that the message of Joe's new image was working. The lifelike hair and beard trend continued until 1976 because of this enormous success.

By now eight basic and talking Adventurer figures were available. An expanding assortment of Adventure sets broadened the toy's versatility. This year GI Joe bagged white tigers, captured pigmy gorillas and even went into space. Sets featuring animals came with some kind of net or trap.

The Adventure Team Fan Club was devised this year to replace the original GI Joe Fan Club. The package for each new GI Joe included an

Adventure Team Club membership folder. The $1.50 enrollment fee provided the member with an official *GI Joe Adventure Team* emblem, a wallet-sized identification card, an Adventure Team iron-on insignia, and a copy of the official GI Joe Adventure Team magazine.

As did its predecessor, the full-color *GI Joe Adventure Team* highlighted the different sets available at toy stores. In a new vein, it featured stories about the A-Team, as well as articles about real-life adventurers such as Thor Heyerdahl (explorer/anthropologist); Neil Armstrong (astronaut); and Jacques Cousteau (marine explorer).

Other items that rounded out the 1970 GI Joe line included the "Dangerous Assignment" Adventure Team game, and a "Color Forms" set. Thanks to these complementary products and the rapidly expanding line of figures and

LEFT:
The black Adventurer addressed the need of a racially diverse marketplace.

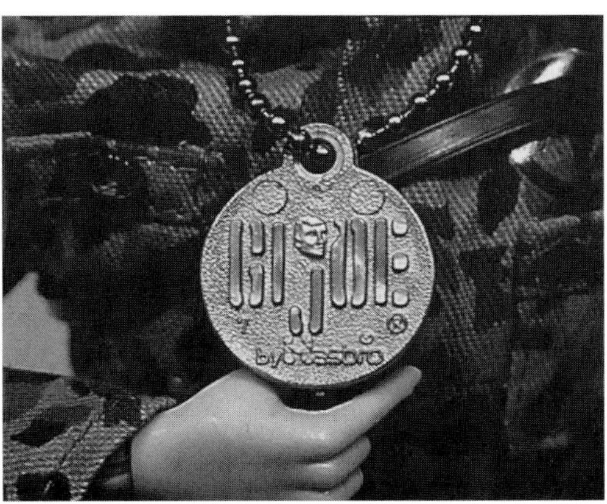

FAR LEFT:
The Adventure Team medallion.

LEFT:
The back of the Adventure Team medallion.

RIGHT: The Fight for Survival set is an excellent example of highly-detailed, true-to-scale design.

accessories, the Hasbro company gained an estimated $7.5 million from its 1970 GI Joe sales.

1971

Amazingly, after 1970's proliferation of figure sets, no new figure sets were released during 1971. There were, however, some "3 in 1 Super Adventure Sets" released, each containing three existing sets in one package, plus a GI Joe Land Adventurer. One of the sets was sold exclusively by Sears.

Hasbro also produced twelve new basic Adventure Team uniform/equipment sets, ranging from the Aerial Recon set to the Secret Agent set. In addition to these sets, the company offered ten new realistic equipment sets, including the Rescue Raft and the Drag Bike.

Many buyers at the 1971 Toy Fair responded favorably to Hasbro's 1971 toy lines, which included 106 new toys and three new product categories. The company was keeping in step with its com-

RIGHT: *Adventure Team* magazine kept GI Joe Club members informed of new developments in the product line.

petitors, it seemed. Thanks, in part, to GI Joe's resurging popularity, the amount of orders at the time of the Toy Fair was more than double the amount at the same time a year ago. Hassenfeld described the turnaround as "beyond belief." With confidence he noted, "The foundation is the important thing, and I think we're building it this year."

1972

Thanks to the sales momentum of 1971, Hasbro's Adventure Team series was expected to rake in record money, especially since the company was producing a large number of new sets for the GI Joe Adventurer. No new GI Joes would be released this year, however, though rival companies were competing with many boys' action figures such as Buddy Charlie, The Baron, Yankee Bravo, and Hombre.

Hasbro issued twelve new and very popular equipment sets for various A-Team figures, including the Underwater Demolition and the Seismograph set. Many equipment pieces had actual working components.

This year marked the premiere of the Mobile Support Vehicle, a two-piece, eight-wheeled excursion vehicle that held two GI Joe Adventurers. The second piece, a detachable headquarters mod-

ABOVE: Members of the new Adventure Team travel in a familiar-looking jeep.

LEFT: The spectacular Mobile Support Vehicle was a large, high-priced piece of equipment.

RIGHT:
Talking figures continued to be introduced, such as this black Talking Adventure Team Commander. This one featured the new lifelike hair.

ule, housed sophisticated communications equipment. This all-terrain vehicle had battery-operated working features, and when assembled measured nearly two feet long. The vehicle sold for $16.99, making it GI Joe's most costly accessory.

This year saw the first Action Playset, known as the GI Joe Adventure Team Headquarters. The headquarters structure had four play areas: a map room, storage room, staging area, and radio shack with signal beacon and buzzer. The unit even boasted an elevator.

A series of GI Joe Adventure Team record albums were produced in 1972 One, a combination book/record set, was released by Peter Pan Records. The jacket held a 33⅓ rpm long-play disc, and an illustrat-

RIGHT:
Before the day of home video cassette players, the book/record combination was an innovative product.

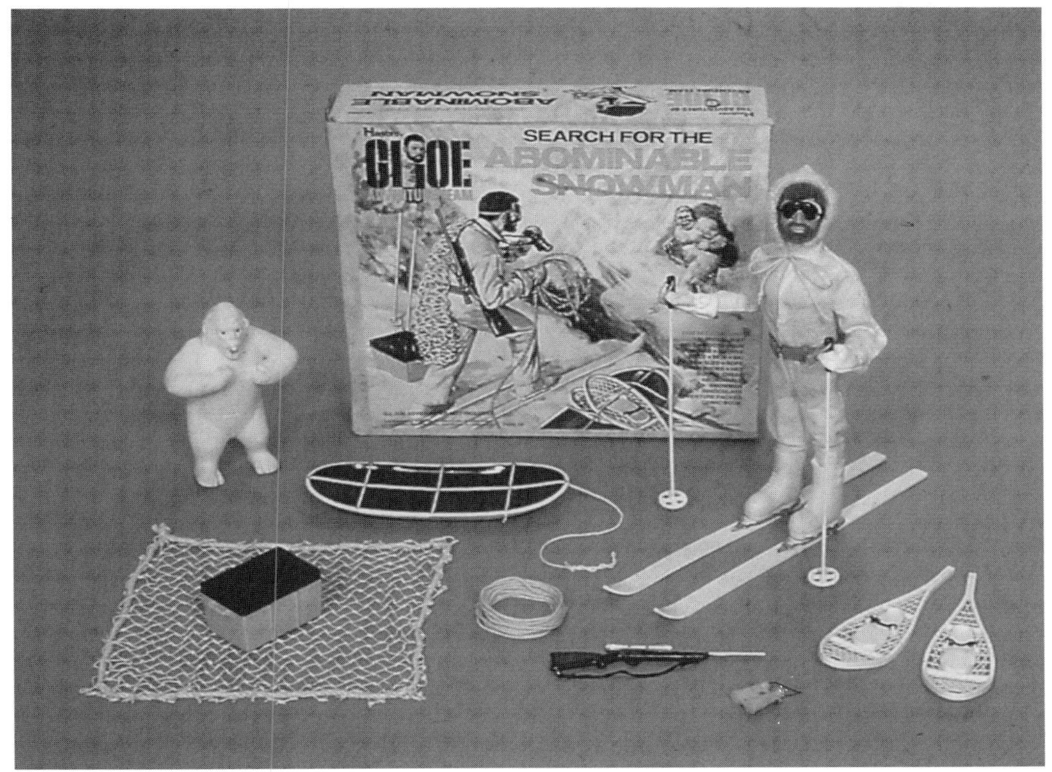

LEFT: The Search for the Abominable Snowman actually included a figure of the mythical monster.

ed read-along comic book. Featured in the book/record set were three GI Joe adventures: "Secret of the Mummy's Tomb"; "Secret Mission to Spy Island"; and "Rescue From Adventure Team Headquarters." A listener could read along in the comic book, turning each page at the sound of a beep.

1973

During this year most of the GI Joe figures and sets from earlier years were still being produced and could be found quite easily on toy store shelves. To expand the selection of GI Joe figures, Hasbro introduced the first black talking Adventure Team Commander (also with lifelike hair and beard). With this new GI Joe, the A-Team was now nine members strong.

Expansion of GI Joe accessories for 1973 was headlined by an ambitious thirteen uniform/equipment sets, ranging from Hidden Treasure to Winter Rescue. As with previous years' sets, these came with a two-piece uniform and a few pieces of gear.

Two larger sets, sold exclusively by Sears, were Search for the Abominable Snowman and Mystery of the Boiling Lagoon. Larger sets such as these generally included an animal to capture, a small vehicle, or even big pieces of equipment.

As for vehicles, this year Hasbro issued its first GI Joe helicopter, built to carry one Adventurer figure. Features included rotor-blade action (hand-turned), and a working winch with cargo hook.

***RIGHT:* This Man of Action had the new Kung-Fu grip, enabling him to grasp objects easily.**

Pressure-sensitive decals (as with many Adventure Team vehicle sets) allowed the owner to add his own trim to the yellow plastic aircraft.

Again, under license, the Irwin company produced a line of vehicles specially designed for Hasbro's Adventure Team. These eight new vehicles were sold only through Sears and J.C. Penney department stores. The series included the All-Terrain Vehicle, Chopper Cycle, Amphibicat, Giant Air-Sea Helicopter, a combat action jeep, Mini-Helicopter, Signal ATV, and a Action Sea Sled. Hasbro also introduced its second playset, the Adventure Team Training Center, touted as "the training ground for the entire Adventure Team." The set featured a 43-inch tower, an obstacle course, a rifle range, a survival tent, a cave, and an adventure booklet.

1974

This year marked another major step in the evolution of the GI Joe figure: Hasbro's unveiling of a GI Joe with the new "Kung-Fu grip." The yet-new Adventure Team Joe was still the same size, still fully posable, and still bore the famous battle scar. But now GI Joe's hands were manufactured from a soft, flexible rubber instead of hard, stiff plastic. The new feature allowed an Adventurer to grasp and hold weapons and tools, hang from branches and cliffs, and even overpower the enemy.

Each model launched from 1970-1973 (with the exception of the talking Astronaut) was reintroduced with this new feature. The Kung-Fu grip, which would be available on almost every model of Adventurer during the next two years, gave sales a noticeable boost—and kept Hasbro's GI Joe ahead of his competition.

Each of the eight different figures with Kung-Fu grip wore outfits identical to earlier issues, but they had one signicant difference in gear. Now, instead of wearing a revolver and shoulder holster, each carried a hunting rifle. Uniform sets offered in 1974 were either totally new or repackaged old models. Hasbro also reissued an assortment of six different equipment sets that first had been marketed in 1972.

The popular green A-Team foot locker was issued again this year, still over one foot long, constructed of durable plastic and complete with equipment lift-out tray and special storage area underneath. This foot locker was packaged with the new Kung-Fu grip GI Joe logo, and wrapped in a different package.

The introduction of GI Joe with the Kung-Fu grip gave occasion for launching a number of popular adventure sets, such as the Devil of the Deep swamp craft and the Sandstorm Survival

ABOVE: The Sea Adventurer displaying his soft, flexible Kung-Fu grip.

Adventure set. As with sets of earlier years, a sixteen-page comic book accompanied each vehicle. Sales of Hasbro's new line was bolstered by dynamic television commercials, demonstrating the unique designs of the adventure sets.

RIGHT:
Mike Powers, Atomic Man, was Hasbro's attempt to capitalize on the popularity of TV's *Six-Million Dollar Man*.

1975

For many years, toys and games related to popular TV shows had been a Hasbro specialty, and GI Joe accessories were no exception. This year, when *Six Million Dollar Man* became a major hit, Hasbro exploited the show's visibility by introducing a "bionic" GI Joe in the likeness of the TV show's lead character, Lee Majors. (At the same time Kenner was marketing a Six Million Dollar Man doll.)

Hasbro's TV-spinoff for the Adventure Team was named Major Mike Powers/Atomic Man. This 11½ inch secret agent figure was man/machine hybrid with a flashing zoom-lens eye, a scar on the *left* side of his face, transparent "atomic" limbs, and rotating Kung-Fu grip hands that controlled a hand-held helicopter rotor.

The Atomic Man came in a camouflage bush jacket and shorts, with instructions for operating his mini-helicopter printed on the all-new blister package. The Atomic Man introduction called for a new line of uniform and equipment sets, bearing names such as Race to Recovery and Command Para Drop.

LEFT:
GI Joe, the all-American action figure.

RIGHT:
A flyer promoting the Adventure Team's Sky Hawk glider.

Some sets included a small vehicle.

Hasbro also produced an Atomic Man Playset called Secret Mountain Outpost. The outpost, disguised as a primitive log cabin, actually housed sophisticated computers and testing equipment.

Super deluxe uniform/equipment sets made for the GI Joe Adventure Team in 1975 included items such as Revenge of Spy Shark and Sky Dive to Danger (featuring a giant spider). Sears offered an exclusive set named Trouble at Vulture Pass, featuring a man-eating vulture. Deluxe sets for this year included four assorted packages, such as Secret Courier and Special Assignment.

Two true-to-scale sets, each with working features, were introduced by Hasbro with the fanfare of nationwide

TV commercials. The first, the Sea Wolf submarine, was a one-man mini-sub. Via remote control the craft could dive, then surface and maintain buoyancy. This set came with a giant squid as well as a full-color adventure booklet.

The second set, the Sky Hawk, was a glider designed to hold one GI Joe Adventurer. Operated much like a kite, the yellow plastic glider with a wingspan of 69 inches launched just as easily. Controlled by a hand-held bobbin and 100 feet of flight line, the Sky Hawk could soar into the air and return slowly to the ground.

1976

To enhance this decade of GI Joe's success, Hasbro created a new variation of the figure, terming it the "Lifelike" GI

LEFT: The new, Lifelike Talking Commander featured fewer moving parts than the previous GI Joe figures.

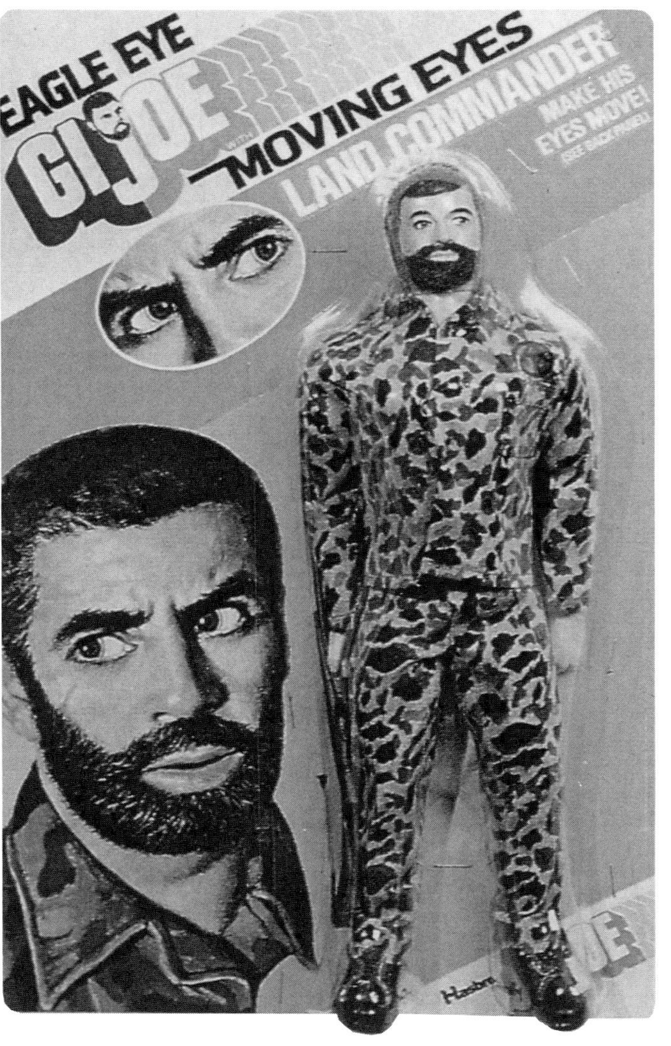

RIGHT: The Eagle-Eye figure had eyes that could be moved from side to side.

youngster. However, in comparison to the rugged construction of the previous GI Joes, this new lifelike figure had limited articulation and durability.

Certain "basic" sets came packaged with the figure wearing only short trunks. Other sets of the same figure included an additional uniform with insignia, boots and also a hunting rifle—for about the same price. Improved blister packages for these sets had the word "new" vividly displayed before the figure's name.

This year Hasbro produced two new versions of the talking Adventure Team Commander, as well as a talking Man of Action,

Joe. All the basic and talking figures of the 1974 cast were reintroduced, each with lifelike hair and beard, battle scar and Kung-Fu grip, but now with only *fifteen* movable parts.

The newly-designed adventurers had a lightweight,muscular plastic body (with molded-on trunks), but all GI Joe's parts were retained by rubber bands. This integrated connecting system reduced the chance of a part accidentally being removed and swallowed by a

each packaged with an extra uniform and equipment. Each talking figure appeared on a blister card within a window display box. With a pull of his dog tag, the GI Joe would issue one of eight adventure commands (different from the original versions).

The new talking figures revealed some distinct design changes. The dog tag now pulled out from the side of the neck instead of the front of the chest, while the sound issued from the back of

the figure instead of the front.

A highly innovative version of GI Joe also was introduced this year by Hasbro. Known as Eagle Eye, the figure was available as Land Commander, Man Of Action and a black Commando. The unique feature of Eagle Eye was his eyes: they moved from side to side by means of a lever at the base of the neck. Now GI Joe was more lifelike than ever before.

Each Eagle Eye, usually packaged on a blister card, wore a complete uniform that included an Adventure Team insignia, boots and hunting rifle. Hasbro promoted Eagle-Eye extensively through nationwide television advertising.

As a complement to Eagle Eye, Hasbro also created two adversary figures, known as Intruders—"strong men from another world." Ads described them as "alien beings who came to wage war on the entire universe. The Intruders were primitive in appearance, only they were highly intellectual beings, cunning and super powerful. A formidable threat to the Adventure Team."

The pair of nine-inch Intruders had rotating heads and featured "Press Action," which enabled their massive crusher arms to "effortlessly destroy" anything in their paths. With the press of a button at the center of his back, an Intruder could grab Eagle Eye—or anything else—in a ruthless bear hug.

The two Intruder models that hit toy stores in 1976 were the Commander (with black molded hair and beard, and gold body armor), and the Warrior (the same figure, but with brown molded hair, no beard, and wearing silver body armor). Each bore a breastplate insignia.

As other rival toy companies introduced superhero action figures (some of which became more widely accepted than GI Joe), Hasbro kept in step with even more new figures. Therefore, in addition to Eagle Eye and Intruders, the company launched Bulletman, "the human bullet." This new GI Joe was

LEFT: Though only nine inches tall, the Intruder characters were an imposing sight.

***RIGHT:* The Land Adventurer, as with the other new, Lifelike GI Joe figures, came with molded-on clothing.**

publicized as "faster than the speed of light, more powerful than a dynamo....Capable of crashing through objects with his steel arms."

Bulletman employed the same design as the lifelike body figures, but had only thirteen movable parts. Rather than the new Kung-Fu grip, he came with hard plastic hands as the original GI Joe did, had black molded hair and a face unlike any other GI Joe. Bulletman wore a silver bullet-shaped helmet, red bodysuit with bullet chest insignia, elastic belt, and boots. Twelve feet of flight line were included, as well as instructions (printed on the package) showing how to secure the string to the figure's back.

No new uniform sets were presented in 1976, but there were new vehicles. The GI Joe Adventure Team gained a newly designed combat four-wheel drive vehicle and trailer. A reissued helicopter with the usual features was again available for the GI Joe Adventure Team with Kung-Fu grip.

For Eagle Eye (and Intruder) fans came the Capture Copter molded in black plastic with pontoons, and the Big Trapper, a yellow tank-like vehicle with a cage in the rear. Both vehicles were to be used by Eagle Eye in apprehending the Intruders. Each vehicle could be purchased with or without an Intruder figure. As an extension of the line of vehicles built for Eagle Eye and the Intruder, Sears offered a set called the Avenger Pursuit Craft, a variation of the Capture Copter.

By now GI Joe fans had a choice of over fifty adventure sets for the Adventure Team. An aggressive onslaught of new TV commercials gave the entire GI Joe line maximum TV exposure, with in-store support from merchandising displays.

After twelve years, Hasbro's GI Joe clearly had vanquished the boys' toy market, but sometimes forces beyond the manufacturer's control can reverse the success of a product. In 1976, that uncontrollable force was the OPEC oil embargo. Petroleum was the major raw material for plastics used to fabricate GI Joe figures, vehicles and most of the equipment. As the cost of petroleum skyrocketed, Hasbro realized it no longer could produce such large figures and sets at a price that the public could afford.

For that and other reasons, company executives decided that GI Joe's domestic marketing should be discontinued. Within days after the public learned of the company's decision, Hasbro had received thousands of letters from boys and girls all over America asking the company not to discontinue their favorite toy. Hasbro executives wondered if they could, somehow, find a way to keep producing GI Joe, but the odds were against them. GI Joe, as we fondly knew him, was shelved.

Later in the year, the Hasbro company introduced the new Defenders action figures. These figures stood 11½ inches tall, just like GI Joe, but they were blow-molded mannequins with limited movement. Each had a rotating head, and arms and legs that pivoted at the shoulders and hips.

RIGHT:
The down-sized Super Joe Commander was a victim of skyrocketing oil prices.

The Defenders were made in GI Joe tradition, but were similar only in size. Each soldier came wearing camouflaged uniform trunks, and was packaged on a blister card. The Defenders line consisted of the basic figure, a few vehicles, and equipment sets. Even though these new figures were not an extension of the GI Joe series, certain GI Joe vehicles, outfits and equipment were used in the line.

Only one version of the Defender soldier was produced this year, selling for about a third the price of the $4.99 basic Adventure Team GI Joe. Vehicle sets included a Defenders four-wheel drive vehicle (reissued from the Adventure Team without searchlight, recoilless rifle and equipment trailer), and a Defenders Iron Knight tank.

As for uniforms and accessories, the Defenders gained six sets, such as Sniper Patrol and Point Man. As expected, many pieces of clothing and gear were reissued Adventure Team items.

Larger Defender series equipment

battery-operated ray gun/communicator, was this year's accessory entry.

A Super Joe Fan Club was inaugurated this year, offering membership at a cost of $1.50. A member received a fold-out poster featuring Super Joe and Gor, and news which included information on the latest equipment available. Other premiums included an iron-on emblem, membership card, Super Joe sticker, wall certificate and special gift offer.

Before the end of 1978, however, the Super Joe series was discontinued, marking the end of Hasbro's extended GI Joe line. Nonetheless, GI Joe soon would be back in action.

ABOVE:
Terron, a monster figure, provided a unique enemy that was vulnerable to light.

CLIP AND MAIL
THIS COUPON TO JOIN
THE SUPER JOE ADVENTURE TEAM
Please enroll me in the Super Joe Adventure Team.
I enclose $1.50 for membership.
Make Check or Money Order payable to Hasbro Industries, Inc.,
(No cash please.) Allow 6 weeks for delivery. Void in states where prohibited by law. (Offer expires June 30, 1979)
SUPER JOE™ ADVENTURE TEAM®
P.O. Box 1288 Pawtucket, R.I. 02862
PLEASE PRINT CLEARLY. YOUR KIT WILL BE SENT TO YOU UNDER THIS MAILING LABEL.
NAME__________
ADDRESS__________
CITY__________ STATE__________
IMPORTANT: ZIP__________
We must have your ZIP CODE to fill your order.

LEFT:
Super Joe Adventure Team, the newest version of the GI Joe Club, used this uniquely shaped application coupon.

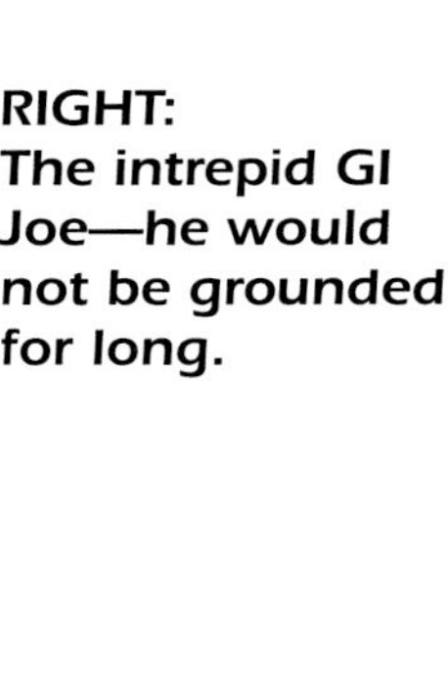

RIGHT:
The intrepid GI Joe—he would not be grounded for long.

CHAPTER FOUR

GI Joe® in the 1980s

1979-1980

Star Wars, the hit movie of 1977, had inspired a new line of *Star Wars* action figures from Kenner. Because the movie had been a hit with both kids and adults, these new figures immediately became a hit when they reached toy stores. The series, launched in 1978, was comprised of versions of all the leading characters in the movie. Their 3¾ inch height set a new standard for action figure size.

Recognizing in the *Star Wars* figures' success a product opportunity, some of the Hasbro executives were laboring secretly to bring about a reintroduction of GI Joe. Bob Prupis, who was vice-president of Boy's Toys, gained the inspiration for a successful concept while watching a hockey game.

Prupis was at a restaurant in Boston, watching a hockey duel between a U.S. and a U.S.S.R. team. Af-

BELOW: *Star Wars* figures from Kenner enjoyed great popularity in the wake of the movie's success.

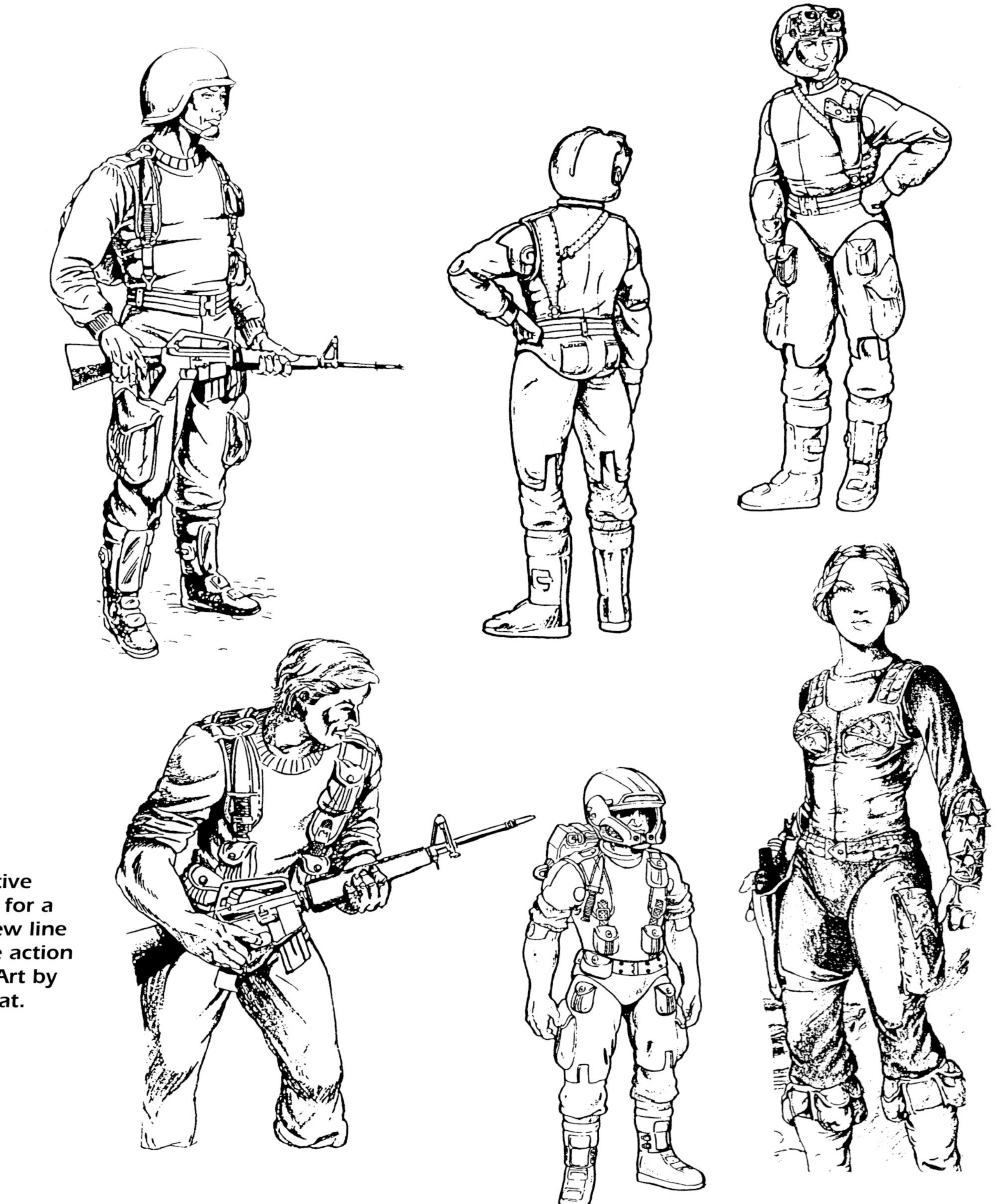

RIGHT: Imaginative sketches for a broad new line of GI Joe action figures. Art by Ron Rudat.

ter winning the game, the U.S. team skated in formation with silver victory cup in hand—and the crowd erupted with a display of flag-waving zeal, even singing patriotic songs.

The emotional charge of that moment gave Prupis the brainstorm he needed. "This was the kind of spirit that I had to capture to bring back GI Joe," he recalls. He would create a patriotic theme, one every American boy would understand. There would be good guys and bad guys, locked in never-ending battle.

The following Monday morning, Hasbro's president, Stephen Hassenfeld, came by Prupis' office and noticed him working feverishly on GI Joe. "Give it a rest," he chided. Hassenfeld saw no promise in trying to reignite the magic of the "old" GI Joe. Nonetheless, Prupis and others continued to develop the concept, and commissioned sketches to be made of a new, down-sized GI Joe.

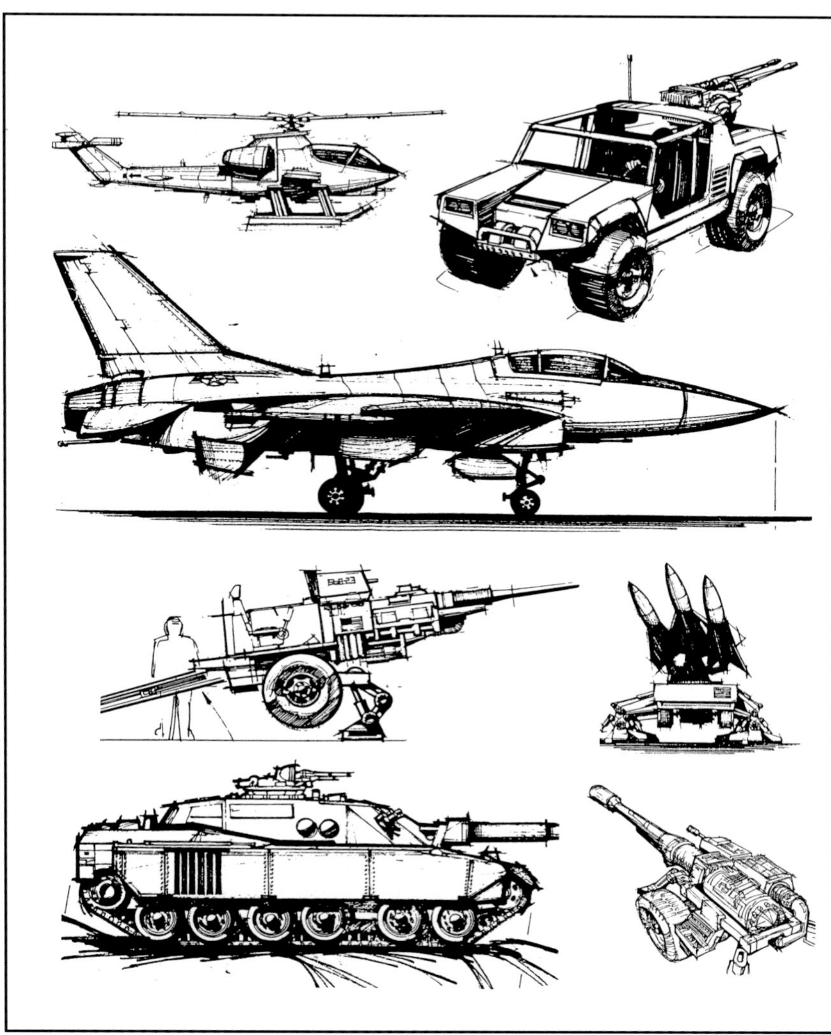

ABOVE: Vehicle concepts for the new GI Joe line reflect a high level of artistic enthusiasm. Art by Wayne Luther.

1981

A few months after Hassenfeld's negative comments about a new GI Joe, Hasbro executives made a second overture to Hassenfeld. The company's advertising agency, Griffin Bacal, presented a new jingle for GI Joe titled, "A Real American Hero," and the concept of a book titled *GI Joe*. Hassenfeld showed only mild interest, but consumer sympathy would soon sway his opinion.

Aware of the public's continuing enthusiasm for the original GI Joe, Hassenfeld began to soften. In response to unrelenting pressure by company employees, the president eventually gave the new GI Joe his enthusiastic support.

Hasbro soon would introduce "GI Joe, a Real American Hero," a line of figures based on the jingle's title. The proposed book became a Marvel comic book, possibly the first book ever advertised on television. (The book's success would lead to an animated se-

RIGHT:
Cobra brought to the GI Joe line the dynamic of an enemy force.

RIGHT:
The Infantry Trooper, code name: Grunt, led the way for the new "pocket size" GI Joe line.

ries.)

According to Kirk Bozigian, a Hasbro vice-president, the revival of GI Joe was only natural. "Toy soldier play is a very important part of a boy's childhood," he observed. "Kids have been playing with soldier figures ever since the Chinese and Egyptian dynasties of 5,000 years ago." As proof, he noted, "In this business, for an action figure like GI Joe to have lasted on the market for almost 30 years is remarkable—when two years is considered a lot."

1982

It seems that old soldiers never die. This year Hasbro reintroduced GI Joe as "A Real American Hero," a new

pocket-sized figure. The new Joe was almost one-third the size of the original version made almost eighteen years earlier.

GI Joe's new size caught on quickly, vaulting him once again to the top of the toy charts, as baby boomers bought for their kids the same toy they once had.

In this incarnation, GI Joe no longer was an individual character, but a team of different commandos, each with a unique name and identity. These characters were duty-bound to defend against the bad guy, who in this case was Hasbro's new Cobra.

Hasbro's new line included nine GI Joes: Stalker, Short Fuse, Breaker, Snake-Eyes, Zap, Flash, Scarlett, Rock 'n Roll and Grunt. The line also included two villains: Cobra and Cobra Officer, members of the enemy army of Cobra Command.

For the new GI Joe's first year, the predominant title on each package was the character's function rather than name, such as Ranger (Stalker), Mortar Soldier (Short Fuse) and Communications Officer (Breaker). The Cobra duo were labeled in similar fashion: Infantry Soldier (Cobra) and Infantry Officer (Cobra Officer). However, as the GI Joe/Cobra line expanded, the actual name of each figure be-

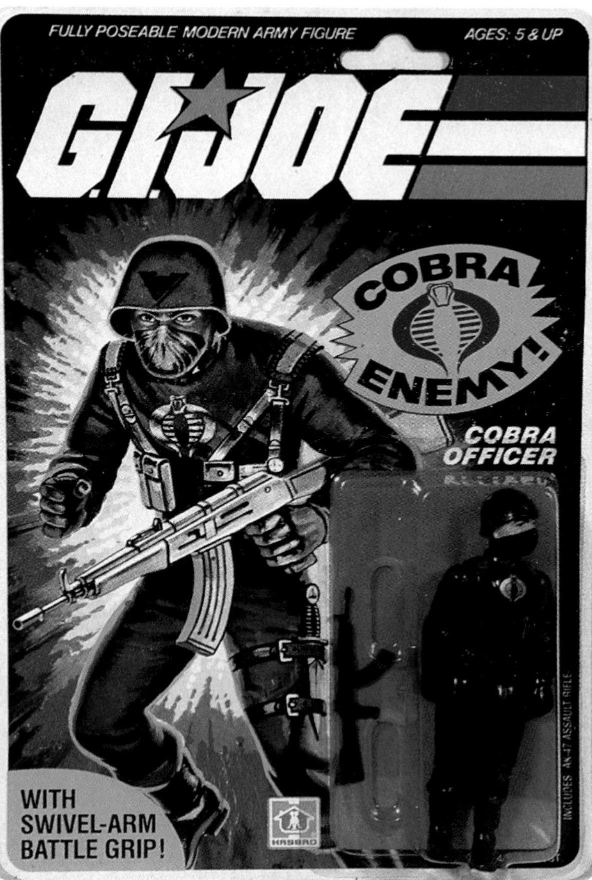

LEFT:
The new Cobra officer was a challenging and colorful arch-rival for GI Joe.

BELOW:
The new GI Joe logo, emphasizing "A Real American Hero," portrays a strongly patriotic theme.

RIGHT: Hasbro made full use of the back of each package, providing information about the enclosed figure, while reminding the owner of other figures in the series.

LEFT:
Flag Point coupons gave GI Joe fans incentive to acquire even more figures and accessories.

came more dominant on the package.

Each figure came with a new, modern uniform that was molded on, making the figure similar to the plastic army men that boys have played with for years. The GI Joe figures had interchangeable snap-on helmets with battle packs and special weapons. Each figure was fully movable and posable.

Each figure and equipment set was packaged on a boldly illustrated, blister pack card, accented by a black background and a red, white and blue logo. The back of each card pictured all the figures available for that year. The back also displayed a command (dossier) file card for the character in the package, listing its name, code name, military specialty, and the equipment required for that specialty.

LEFT:
Trading cards from Impel gave enthusiasts a new way to enjoy GI Joe.

**RIGHT:
Hasbro took full advantage of GI Joe's popularity by offering licenses to produce a wide array of products, including plastic adhesive bandages.**

This was the first year all art for GI Joe packaging was created in-house by Hasbro.

The new GI Joe figures were manufactured first in Hong Kong, then in China. The entire process, from concept to design to production, usually took about a year. The cycle for vehicles required about a year and a half, because of the detailed mechanics in each design.

The average GI Joe figure in the Real American Hero line usually retailed for $2.49 each, with vehicle sets ranging from $3.99 to $14.99. To promote the collectibility of the GI Joe line, Hasbro offered special promotions and giveaways through the year. Each GI Joe toy carried "Flag Points," good for special premiums. Kids could clip and save these points, then redeem them for GI Joe products. During this year,

Cobra Commander was available for five Flag Points and $1.75 for postage.

Four GI Joe equipment packs were offered during this premier year. One, the Jet Pack (JUMP), included a laser blaster and launch pad. It also had a refueling console with advanced communications capabilities.

The Attack Cannon (also known as FLAK) helped to defend the Mobile Strike Force Team from tank or plane attacks. Its simulated howitzer, on folding legs, could elevate and swivel, and could be knocked down and transported.

The Heavy Artillery Laser (HAL) was the GI Joe army's top secret weapon system. It offered ultra-modern design with twin-barreled lasers that rotated 360 degrees and elevated 45 degrees. Included with this set was the GI Joe figure Grand Slam.

The Mobile Missile System (MMS) boasted three missiles that could rotate and elevate. The unit could be towed into action by the VAMP or MOBAT, new vehicles in the GI Joe line.

The new GI Joe's vehicles featured futuristic designs. The Rapid Fire Motorcycle Attack Vehicle (RAM)included a detachable 20mm Vulcan Gatling cannon, side car, and twin saddle bags.

The Attack Cannon (VAMP) was the latest in rapid-fire, four-wheel-drive, all-terrain vehicles. The plastic ATV could serve both as a transport and attack vehicle. Its twin machine guns, that swiveled and elevated, were operated by the figure Clutch.

The ultimate GI Joe action vehicle was the Motorized Battle Tank (MOBAT) based on the U.S. Army's most advanced designs. Its highly detailed body, with grilles, hatches and tools, was propelled by a battery-powered motor via tank treads. Other features included a simulated infrared search beam, rotating turret.

BELOW: The GI Joe Medic, code name: Doc, came equipped with a stretcher and flare launcher.

RIGHT:
A close-up view of the new swivel-arm battle grip.

Each vehicle (and weapon system) came with a detailed diagram (on the back of the instruction sheet) explaining how the real-life version of the unit would operate.

To promote the new line, Hasbro revived the fan club concept, offering membership in the GI Joe Mobile Strike Force Team. Hasbro also blitzed the airwaves with six commercials on network and local television throughout the country.

In addition to action figures and accessories, Hasbro released items such as GI Joe paint or pencil by numbers sets. The pencil set contained six pictures and six colored pencils. The paint set offered two 8 x 10-inch pictures and six acrylic paints, as well as a paintbrush.

An aggressive GI Joe licensing program had, by year's end, secured nearly 50 licensing agreements to manufacture GI Joe-related products. For example, Garan Industries introduced a line of boys' clothes based on GI Joe; King Seeley made Thermos/lunch kits; the Marvel Comics Group published *GI Joe, A Real American Hero* comic books; and Family Home Entertainment offered video cassettes. Even a GI Joe breakfast cereal was being marketed. The appeal of GI Joe's license was so powerful that leading computer hardware and software manufacturers as well as publishers would be utilizing it.

This sudden expansion of products inspired a new generation of young enthusiasts to obtain and collect these modern GI Joe figures. Even collectors of the original full-sized series have shown interest in the down-sized Joe. The GI Joe phenomenon was alive again.

BELOW: The Cobra Enemy Weapons Supplier, code name: Destro, was a popular character in the series.

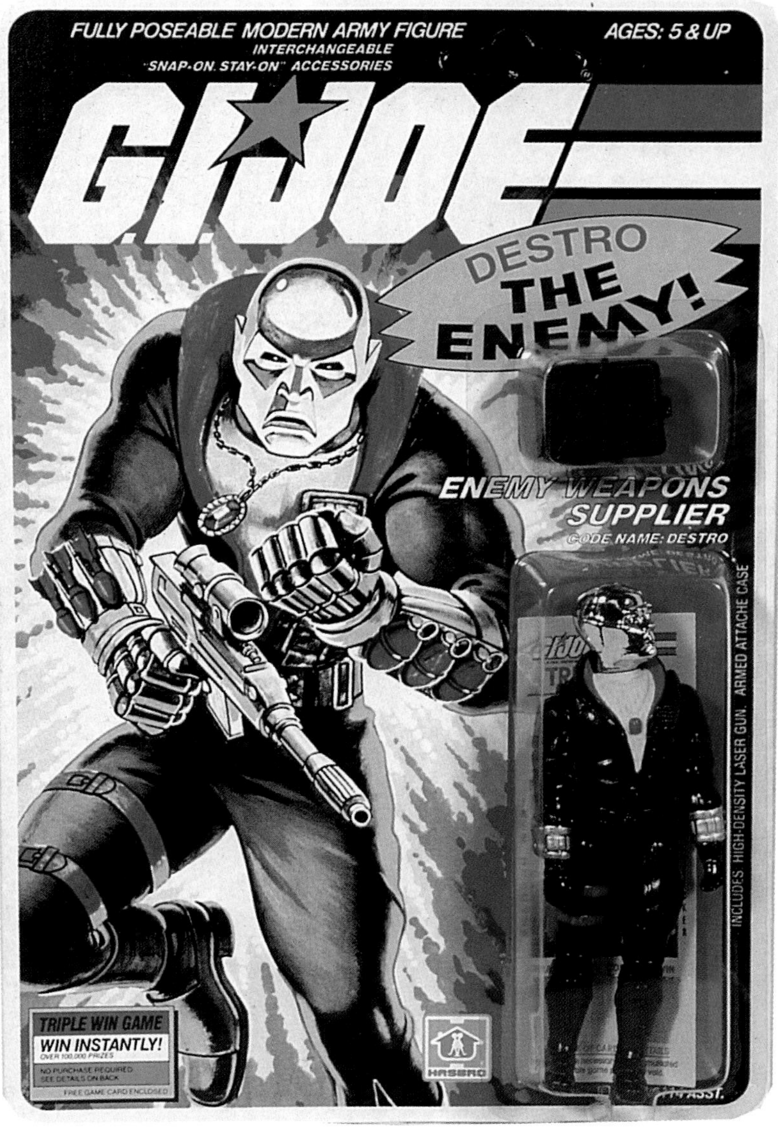

1983

The TV ads touting the "Real American Hero" jingle were a significant reason for the success of the new GI Joe. Such television advertising is standard fare today for marketing the GI Joe line. (Hasbro was a pioneer in TV toy promotion, claiming their 1952 commercial for Mr. Potato Head to have been the first televised toy ad.)

Of GI Joe commercials in the 1990s, Kirk Bozigian has said, "We decided we wanted something that would bring the toys to life. We wanted to do a commercial that was like a GI Joe movie [using] live actors in a series of ads that tell a bit of a story and have cliff-hanging endings."

Characters produced in 1982 had straight arms which could bend only at the shoulder and elbow joints. In 1983, however, GI Joe and Cobra gained the "swivel-arm battle grip." With this feature a figure's arms could rotate 360 degrees just above the elbow joint, thus making it possible to hold weapons and equipment in a more realistic manner. The figures of 1982 were reissued with the swivel-arm battle grip.

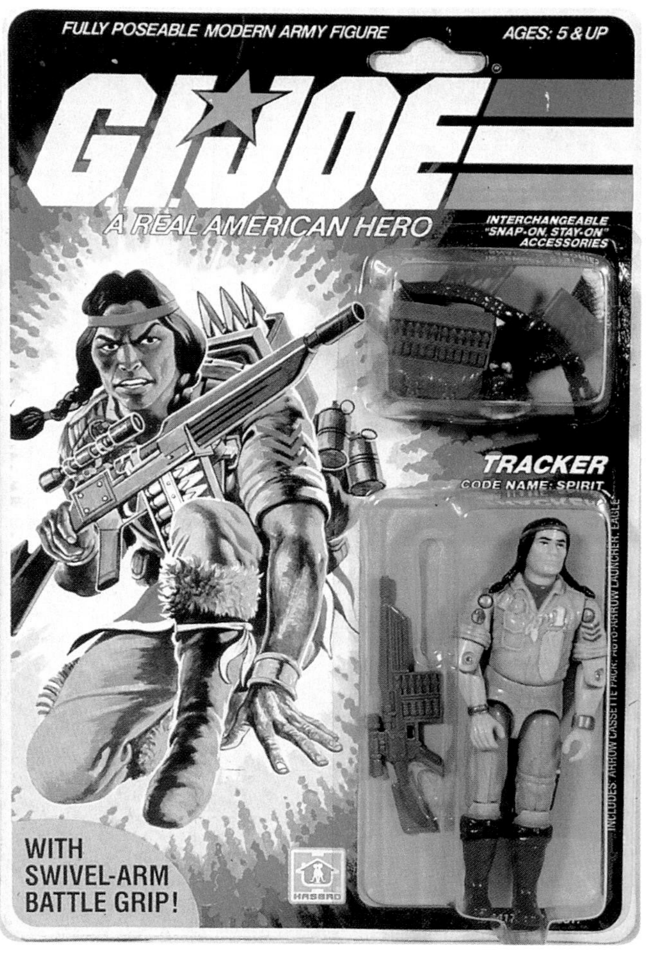

RIGHT: Tracker, code name: Spirit, brought a Native American character to the forefront

Seven GI Joe specialists were introduced this year, the first six being Tripwire, Airborne, Snow Job, Torpedo, Gung-Ho and Doc, with each selling for $2.25. The seventh, the Master Sergeant named Duke, was the first mail-order figure available directly from Hasbro. Duke was available for free if a customer sent in three Flag Points. The Cobra enemy series added two new figures, Major Bludd and Destro.

Many of these "new" GI Joe figures were manufactured with molds from previously released figures. Just as the figures of the 1960s and 70s, many of them were virtually identical to each other. The use of existing character molds was a cost-efficient

way to produce more figures.

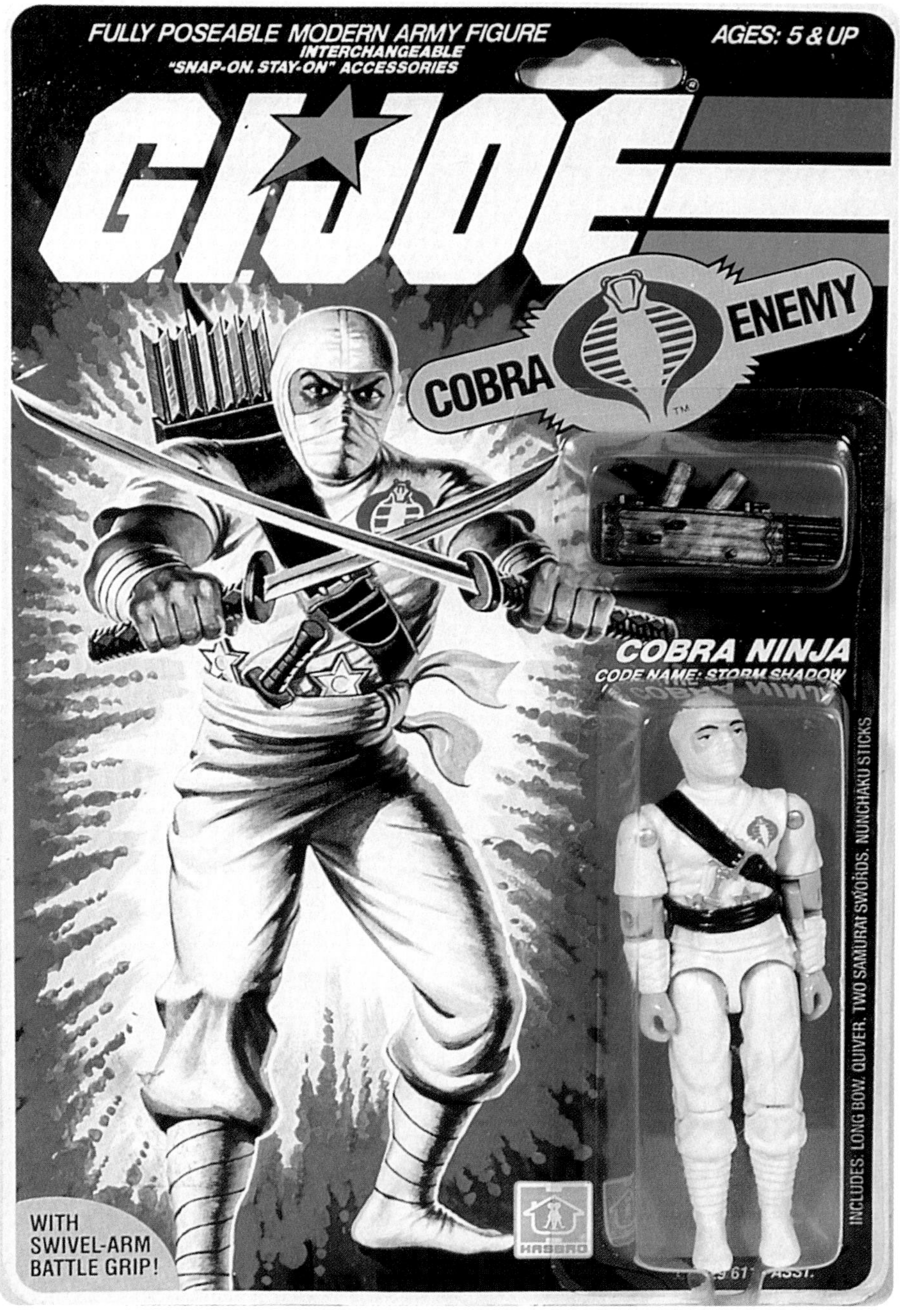

The GI Joe Mobile Strike Force Team gained six vehicle sets: Dragon Fly XH-1; Sky Striker XP-14F; Wolverine; Polar Battle Bear; an amphibious personnel carrier; and the Falcon glider. Two of the three Cobra vehicles were the HISS tank and the FANG glider.

Accessory packages for GI Joe included sets such as JUMP with Grand Slam. A Pac Rats assortment offered a flamethrower, machine gun and missile launcher. The first Battle Gear Accessory Pack was introduced this year. Cobra equipment included one set called SNAKE, which was battle armor that snapped over Cobra.

Two display sets were offered for the GI Joe and Cobra series. The first was the Pocket Patrol Pack, which could hold three figures and clip onto a belt. The second was a collector's display case, a plastic container large enough to accommodate twelve figures along with the command file card for each.

This year two playsets were introduced. For the GI Joe team came the Headquarters Command Center, a weapons-laden fortress. The unit contained movable surveillance cameras, search lights, machine guns, and a cannon that could pivot in any direction. There was even a section for command file cards.

For Cobra, exclusively from Sears, came the Cobra Missile Command Headquarters. Similar to the GI Joe version, this item came with three figures: Cobra Officer, Cobra Soldier and Cobra Commander.

Also for 1983, the first GI Joe cartoon mini-series was broadcast on New York's WPIX during September. Shown in five parts, the syndication

ABOVE: Cobra Ninja, code name: Storm Shadow, brought a new fighting concept to the GI Joe world.

featured show titles such as "The MASS Device" and "The Stake in the Serpent's Heart." The mini-series also was shown as a 100-minute television movie. The video cassette, available from Family Home Entertainment, was titled *GI Joe, Real American Hero.*

1983-1984

Hasbro's GI Joe line of action figures was now at the top of the charts, among the year's five best-selling toys. The 1982 and 1983 series still were available, and twelve figures would be released in the 1983-1984 series.

Kids could choose from seven new figures in the GI Joe team: Mutt with Junkyard, Spirit with Freedom, Rip-Cord, Road Block, Recondo, Blow Torch, and Duke. For the Cobra team came five characters: Baroness, Storm Shadow, Scrap Iron, Fire-Fly, and a special mail-order Cobra Commander with hood. Each basic figure set sold for $2.25. (GI Joe and Cobra figures from 1982 were not available this year. Generally, a figure was available only for a two-year period before its removal from the line.)

Vehicles in this two-year series included six sets for GI Joe and five for Cobra. Of special note was GI Joe's Killer WHALE, an armored Hovercraft vehicle with twin elevating cannons, two rotating machine guns and six depth charges. The craft's four casters allowed it to "hover" on a flat surface. The vehicle carried up to nine figures and included the driver Cutter.

Other vehicles issued for Joe were the SHARC with Deep-Six; the VAMP Mark II with Clutch; the Slugger with Thunder; the Sky Hawk; and a Sears exclusive, the VAMP four-wheel drive vehicle with HAL. The Cobra vehicle sets included Rattler, an attack plane; Stinger, a night attack four-wheel drive vehicle; Water Moccasin, a swamp boat; and Swamp Skier.

Battle Gear Accessory Pack #2 became available this year, containing a variety of helmets, backpacks and weapons in all new colors. Also included were battle figure stands that helped position the figures.

Three Battlestation Assortment sets were produced this year. These mini-playsets with accessories were: Bivouac, Watchtower and Mountain Howitzer. Other equipment packages were a missile defense unit, machine gun defense unit and a mortar defense unit.

Mail-order items included two authentically detailed vehicle sets. One, a Marine Assault Nautical Air-Driven Transport (MANTA), cost one Flag Point and $1.25 for shipping. The other was the Parachute set, available for one Flag Point and $1.50 for shipping.

Other Cobra equipment for the 1983/1984 series included three sets. First was the Assault System Pod (ASP), a vehicle with a cockpit, and turret with a rotating cannon. Two other sets were the Covert Light Aerial Weapon (CLAW), a one-man flying weapon that housed a machine gun, Flashfire bombs and two venom rockets; and the System Neutralizer-Armed Kloaking

LEFT:
Lady Jaye proved to be one of the most popular female action figures in the GI Joe line.

RIGHT: The mirror-image Crimson Guard Commanders, Tomax and Xamot, provided a way to gain two action figures in one package

Equipment (SNAKE), a suit that attaches to Cobra and brainwashes GI Joe.

Presented during the 1983/1984 series was a die cast vehicle set, containing metal replicas of GI Joe's weapons and vehicles. One set was a three-piece package that included GI Joe's rapid-fire motorcycle (RAM), heavy artillery laser (HAL) and the attack vehicle (VAMP), all for $7.99. These could be purchased separately for $2.59 each. Also available were the attack cannon (FLAK), the battle tank (MOBAT) and the mobile missile system (MMS).

A new underwater accessory line this year offered a swim mask, snorkel and swim fins that could be purchased individually or in combination sets. In 1984 Hasbro added swim goggles to the line.

1984

Each year a new action/adventure theme was developed, and new GI Joe and Cobra figure sets continued to expand the line. During 1984, GI Joe fans were favored with over twenty new characters. For the GI Joe series came figures such as Flint; Snake-Eyes with Timber; Bazooka; Air Tight; Lady Jaye; Quick Kick; Dusty; Alpine; Footloose; Barbecue; and Shipwreck with his parrot.

The figure Tripwire was reissued this year in a Listen'n Fun pack, which included a story cassette that detailed the entire adventure. The complete set sold for $3.75.

New Cobra enemies from Hasbro included Tomax and Xamot; Buzzer;

LEFT:
Cobra Frogman, code name: Eels, posed an underwater threat to the Real American Hero.

BELOW:
Dreadnok, code name: Torch, was the beginning of a new series of Dreadnoks enemies.

RIGHT:
The package for Polar Assault, code name: Snow Serpent, promised a chance at big prizes.

Ripper; Torch; Tele-Viper; Eels; Snow Serpent; and the Crimson Guard—the intelligence behind Cobra. The Crimson Guard Commanders, Tomax and Xamot, were mirror-image twins. A new enemy, Dreadnoks, also was introduced this year. A "Triple Win Game" promotional giveaway was included inside all figure sets.

For GI Joe, the year's outstanding vehicle set was a 7-foot long aircraft carrier named the USS Flagg, with admiral figure Keel-Haul. It sold for a whopping $89.99. Other vehicle sets were the Mauler with Heavy-Metal; Bridge Layer with Toll-Booth; the AWE Striker with Crankcase; Snowcat with Frostbite; Silver Mirage Motorcycle; and Armadillo Mini-Tank.

For the Cobra enemy, new vehicle sets included the Hydrofoil with the Lamprey's Pilot, and the Ferret all-terrain vehicle. Sears offered two exclusive Cobra vehicle sets, the Sentry and Missile System (SMS), and the Motorized Crimson Attack Tank— a reissued

ABOVE: Unique, exciting vehicles continued to expand the GI Joe line, as characterized by the Silver Mirage Motorcycle set.

LEFT: A special "free" Sergeant Slaughter offer was featured on the package for GI Joe Commander, code name: Hawk.

version of the MOBAT with all new colors.

This year brought four Battlefield and Battlestation Assortments: Ammo Dump, Forward Observer, Check Point and Air Defense. The Battle Gear Accessory Pack #3, as #2, contained helmets, backpacks and weapons in all new colors, with battle stands for posing figures.

Cobra enemy gear and equipment included a weapons assortment Flight Pod, a one-man bubble craft for surveying GI Joe from above. From the Battlefield Vehicles Assortment came the heavily armed Nightlanding Raft, and from the Battlefield Accessory Assortment came the Rifle Range.

A GI Joe playset introduced in 1984 was the Tactical Battle Platform. The set featured multi-level battle platforms and heli-pad, and was armed with a rotating radar-guided cannon and surface-to-air missiles.

A second GI Joe cartoon mini-series was aired for five week nights during September of this year. Episodes sported lurid titles such as "In the Cobra's Pit" and "Amusement Park of Terror." The shows again were compiled as a 100-minute video cassette, titled *GI Joe Volume 2: The Revenge of Cobra*, and distributed by Family Home Entertainment.

1985

This year GI Joe sales reached new heights. The popular series was ranked the best-selling toy in America by *Toy and Hobby World*, a toy trade magazine.

Until now, each GI Joe figure's head could turn only from left to right. For 1985 Hasbro's engineers designed a ball and socket neck assembly which enabled the head to swivel fully. This new feature, however, was available only on new characters. Even reissued figures from prior years would not receive the new neck design.

ABOVE: Zandar, and siblings Zartan and Zarana, were members of a unique enemy family.

Twelve new GI Joe figures joined the line in 1985: Leather Neck; Low-Light; Main Frame; Beach Head; Life-Line; Ice Berg; Sci-Fi; Wet-Suit; Dial-Tone; Road-Block and Hawk (reissued from earlier years); and Sergeant Slaughter (available by mail order).

Toys "R" Us marketed a special set named "Special Mission: Brazil." The pack included five figures: Claymore, Dial-Tone, Wet-Suit, Leather-Neck and Main Frame, and included a cassette tape that detailed the secret mission.

Six Cobra enemy figures were premiered this year: BAT, Zandar (Zartan's brother), Monkey Wrench, Dr. Mindbender, Zarana, and Viper. Zarana (Zartan's sister), one of the many females in the series, came in two versions, the first with a larger head and earrings, and the second with a smaller head and no earrings. Some of these figures, such as Zartan's Chameleon, the Dreadnok Swampfire, and Dreadnok Air and Ground Assault sets had body parts that changed color in sunlight.

BELOW & RIGHT: Duke and Zartan Paint-A-Figurine sets gave GI Joe enthusiasts a unique way to creatively enjoy their hobby.

Vehicles for GI Joe included six all-new sets. The Tomahawk with Lift-Ticket; HAVOC with Cross-Country; Conquest X-30 with Slip-Stream; and Triple-T with Sgt. Slaughter; Devil Fish; and LVC Recon sled.

Seven Cobra vehicles for this year's series included the Night Raven S-3P with Strato-Viper; the Stun with Motor-Viper; the Dreadnok

Thunder Machine with Thrasher; the Air Chariot with Serpentor the Cobra Emperor; and the Dreadnok Swamp-Fire. Sears sold two Dreadnok vehicles: the Air Assault vehicle and the Ground Assault vehicle.

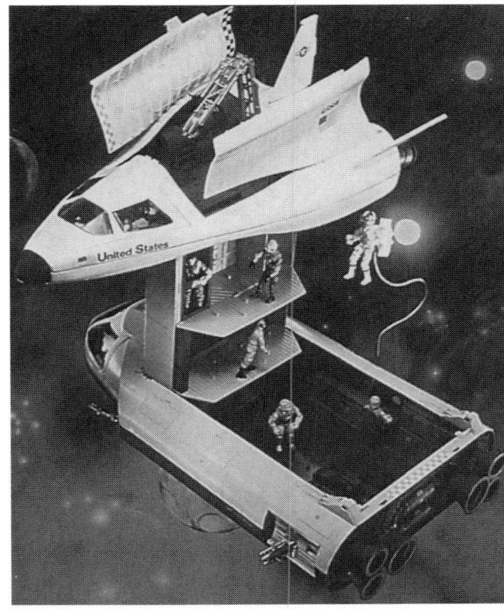

LEFT: The Defiant Space Shuttle Launch Complex, shown in a catalog photo, was both authentic and pricey—$99.99.

for two different radio frequencies, so two vehicles could be operated in the same location. The set sold for $54.99.

Smaller vehicles included the Persuader, a ten-wheeled attack vehicle with driver Back Stop; and the Road Toad and the Coastal Defender from the Battlefield Vehicles Assortment.

For Cobra, vehicles included the Buzz Boar, an underground attack unit; the Mamba, a supersonic attack helicopter with pilot Gyro-Viper; the Maggot, three vehicles in one with driver WORMS; the Wolf, a swift winter attack vehicle with missiles and ski torpedoes, including driver Ice-Viper; the Cobra Sea Ray underwater attack and aerial reconnaissance vehicle, with driver Sea Slug; and Pogo, the Ballistic Battle Ball, a one-man attack vehicle. For the Dreadnoks there were two sets: Air Skiff, with Zanzibar the Pirate Leader; and Dreadnok Cycle with a gunner station.

A new series of vehicle equipment sets, the first being Vehicle Gear Accessory Pack #1, was added to the line. The pack contained weapons, Snow Cat Ski-Pedoes, and more.

Introduced this year were eight GI Joe and Cobra Motorized Action Packs. For GI Joe there was the Anti-Aircraft Gun; Helicopter Pack; Radar Station; and Rope Walker. Cobra packs included Rope Crosser; Earth Borer; Mountain Climber; and Pom-Pom Gun Pack. Each had a wind-up motor, moving actions, an on/off switch, and it converted into a backpack.

Other equipment included the Strategic Long-Range Artillery Machine (SLAM), an aircraft vehicle with multi-bar-

RIGHT: This catalog photo displays the fighting vehicle, Persuader, an excellent example of aggressive, futuristic styling.

RIGHT: Spearhead's unique pet was named Max—a bobcat.

reled guns, cannon missiles and more; and Battle Gear Accessory Pack #5, a collection of more helmets, rifles, backpacks and battle stands.

Playsets included Mobile Command Center, a three-level mobile fortress with Missile Command Center operator Steam Roller. The center was actually a command vehicle with service, command and missile bays, and armed with high-tech weaponry. It cost $34.

The fourth GI Joe cartoon mini-series aired in September 1986, again in five parts. The second full GI Joe cartoon series aired the same year with over thirty episodes, such as "Last Hour to Doomsday" and "Into Your Tent I Will Silently Creep."

The fifth cartoon mini-series aired in June 1987. The show originally was broadcast as a 2½ hour TV movie titled, *GI Joe: The Movie*, and later was used in the regular cartoon series. It also was available on video cassette from Celebrity Home Entertainment/Celebrity.

As part of its public relations strategy, Hasbro conducted the first GI Joe "Search for Real American Heroes." This national awards program honored boys and girls for heroic deeds, such as exhibiting courage or compassion in a life-saving situation, doing meritorious community service, or achieving a personal goal despite adversity.

1988

Twelve new GI Joe characters were made this year. They included Blizzard; Repeater; Shockwave; Charbroil; Hit and Run; Lightfoot; Hardball; Spearhead and Max; Budo; and a reissued Storm Shadow, each selling for $2.55. Hasbro offered Starduster, with

ABOVE: The new Battleforce 2000 garnered extra visibility with this double-figure set, containing Maverick and Blocker.

a Pocket Patrol figure carrying case, for $3.50 plus two Flag Points. In addition, Target stores exclusively were carrying Hit and Run with the Airborne Assault parachute and pack.

Battleforce 2000 was an "elite experimental assault unit" that used prototype vehicles in its mission to defeat Destro and his Iron Grenadiers. The set introduced figures such as Avalanche and Blaster, Maverick with Blocker, Dodger, and Knockdown.

The new Tiger Force figure set included the reissued characters Duke, Roadblock, Dusty, Flint, Bazooka, Tripwire, and Lifeline. This seven-man combat team conducted surprise attacks on unsuspecting enemy troops with the force of a tiger. Each figure came packaged with combat accessories, accented with a tiger stripe motif.

Six Night Force packs were sold only at Toys "R" Us. Each carded set contained two GI Joe action figures with weapons. The sets included figures such as Lt. Falcon and Sneek-Peek; Outback and Crazy Legs; Psych-Out and Tunnel Rat; Repeater and Charbroil; Shockwave and Lightfoot; and Spearhead and Muskrat.

Target also offered a special "2-in-1 Pack." The GI Joe/Cobra set, named Ultimate Enemies, contained the GI Joe character Muskrat and Cobra enemy Voltar, each with specialized weapons.

Seven Cobra figures debuted this year, including Iron Grenadier; Toxo-

RIGHT: New sets abounded, including Tiger Force, which featured colorful characters such as desert fighter Dusty.

RIGHT: Voltar, Destro's General, was a dramatic figure in the Iron Grenadiers series.

LEFT: The Cobra Toxo-Viper looked as fearsome as his name sounded.

Viper; Astro-Viper; Hydro-Viper; Voltar; and Road Pig. (The Iron Grenadier figure, was the first of a complete army called the Iron Grenadiers.) Two Flag Points and $1 would buy Super Trooper, made of metallized plastic. Both Cobra and GI Joe figures enjoyed more accessories this year than ever before.

RIGHT:
Charbroil and Repeater helped to debut the new Nightforce.

LEFT: This catalog photo captures the hostile look of the Mean Dog battle vehicle.

The product line gained twelve vehicles this year, including the eight-wheeled Rolling Thunder missile launcher tank with driver Armadillo; the Phantom X-19 stealth fighter with pilot Ghostrider; Mean Dog with Wild Card; Warthog; Skystorm with Windmill; Swamp Masher; Desert Fox with Skidmark; the RPD; and Locust Bomber.

Vehicles for the Battleforce 2000 included sets such as the Marauder, a two-man motorcycle tank; Sky Sweeper; Vindicator; Dominator; Eliminator; and Vector Jet, a fighter with laser cannon, bombs, and laser guns. Each Battleforce vehicles sold for $6.49.

Five Tiger Force vehicle sets were launched in 1988: the Tiger Paw, a tracked vehicle with missiles, a side-mounted laser cannon and nose gun; Tiger Shark; the Tiger Cat with Frostbite; the Tiger Fly with Recondo; and the Tiger Rat plane with turbo fan engines, nose-mounted rotating laser cannon, dual machine guns, and fourteen missiles on the Tiger Rat.

Toys "R" Us sold an exclusive line of

RIGHT:
Marvel issued a special comic book to mark GI Joe's twenty-fifth birthday.

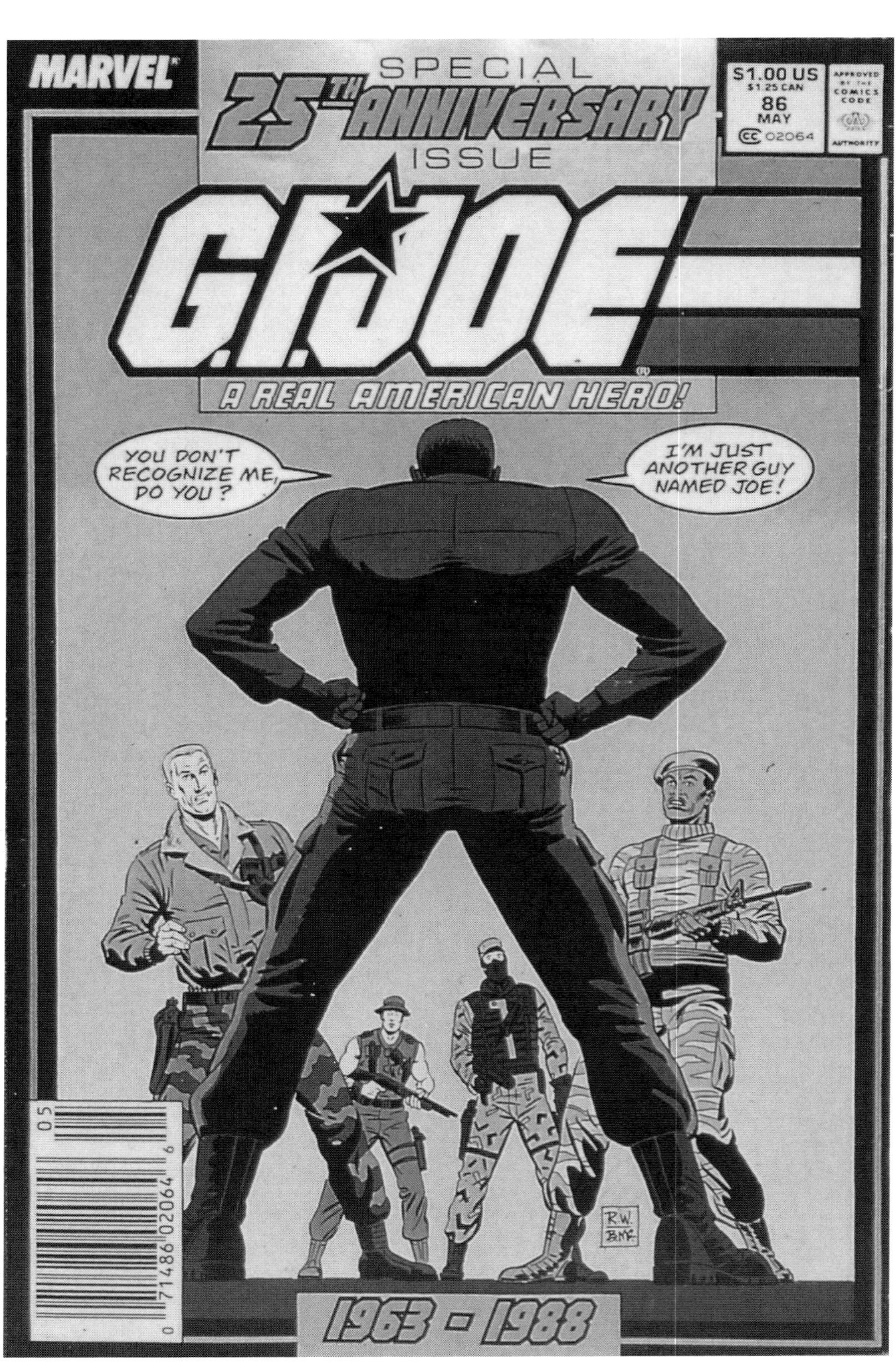

six GI Joe Night Force vehicles: the Night Storm; Night Blaster; Night Raider; Night Shade; Night Striker; and the Night Scrambler. Each Night Force vehicle had glow-in-the-dark battle labels.

Hasbro offered six Cobra vehicle sets: the Bugg, an amphibious command vehicle with a removable two-man Hovercraft submarine with twin cannons, machine guns, anti-aircraft gun, and two missiles, with driver Secto Viper; the Iron Grenadiers-Battleforce 2000 DEMON with Ferret; the Despoiler with Destro; a VTOL plane; Stellar Stilletto with Star-Viper; and the Iron Grenadiers AGP (anti-gravity pod) with pilot Nullifier.

Motorized Vehicle Packs for GI Joe included the Tank Car, Scuba Pack, and ATVs. Packs for Cobra included the Gyro Copter, Rocket Sled, and Scuba Pack.

Motorized Action Packs for GI Joe totaled six sets. For GI Joe came the Mine Sweeper, Mortar Launcher, and Double Machine Gun. For Cobra the Dreadnok Battle Ax, Twin Missile Launcher, and Machine Gun Nest.

Equipment-carrying vehicles for the Cobra enemy line included the Imp, an armored rocket launcher; the Adder, a six-wheeled missile-launcher; and the Battle Barge, a floating gun emplacement. Additional equipment for Cobra included the Battle Gear Accessory Pack #6.

New playsets for Hasbro's GI Joe Team included the Battleforce 2000 Future Fortress which contained six Battleforce vehicles: Vector Jet; Dominator Snow Tank; Marauder motorcycle tank; Sky Sweeper anti-aircraft tank; Vindicator Hovercraft; and the Eliminator four-wheel drive vehicle.

Since the GI Joe team's introduction in 1982, Hasbro reportedly had sold over $600 million in related mer-

BELOW: Sergeant Slaughter, patterned after the professional wrestler, received special attention during the twenty-fifth anniversary.

RIGHT:
An offer of free face camouflage was an incentive to buy GI Joe figures.

FREE
INSIDE
FACE CAMOUFLAGE

Caution: Keep away from eye area.

©1988 Hasbro, Inc. all rights reserved. Distributed by Hasbro, Inc. Pawtucket, RI 02862

Active ingredients: Water, isopropyl palmitate, propylene glycol, mineral oil (and) lanolin alcohol, stearic acid, isostearyl neopentanoate, glyceryl stearate, cetyl alcohol, triethanolamine, peg-40-stearate, lecithin, magnesium aluminum silicate, imidazolidinyl urea, cellulose gum, dimethicone, methylparaben, propylparaben.

May contain: Titanium dioxide, iron oxides, chromium oxide green, ultramarine blue and ultramarine violet.

Net wt. .034 oz.

chandise. According to one estimate, in 1986 alone two GI Joe figures had been sold for every boy in the United States between the ages of five and twelve.

1988-1989

As GI Joe's twenty-fifth anniversary approached, retail sales for the line were approaching the billion dollar mark. A Hasbro survey taken during the late 1980s showed that two out of every three boys between the ages of five and eleven owned a GI Joe series action figure.

February 9, 1989 was GI Joe's twenty-fifth birthday, and a big anniversary celebration was held at Hasbro's showroom in New York City. Every New York TV station, and virtually every local newspaper covered the event. The Marvel Comics Group published a twenty-fifth anniversary issue to commemorate the occasion. Professional wrestler Sgt. Slaughter, recently appointed as the spokesperson for the GI Joe ad campaign, was the main attraction at the celebration. A figure bearing his name and likeness would

RIGHT:
GI Joe exhibits his Kung-Fu grip at the Smithsonian Institution.

ABOVE: Mutt, and his attack dog, represent the new series Slaughter's Marauders.

LEFT: Underwater diving is a recurring theme in GI Joe sets, and Deep Six was this year's version.

be the leader of an all-new series named Slaughter's Marauders.

GI Joe's reputation had spread even to the nation's repository of history. From July 1989 to March 1991, the Smithsonian Institution featured an exhibit called "Men and Women—A History of Costume, Gender and Power," in which a 1974 GI Joe with Kung-Fu grip represented the action/adventure figure series.

During this momentous year GI Joe gained nine new characters: Recoil, Scoop, Count Down, Snake-Eyes, Rock 'n Roll, Stalker, Back Blast, Downtown, and Deep Six. Each series figure

RIGHT:
The package for this Battleforce 2000 character, Dee-Jay, included a free Micro Figure.

sold for $2.55. A free one-inch micro-figure was included with each series figure. The GI Joe Battleforce 2000 also added one figure: laser trooper—code name Dee Jay.

The new Slaughter's Marauders combat unit offered six figures, plus two animals. Choices included: Sgt. Slaughter; Mutt and Junkyard; Low-Light; Spirit and Freedom; Barbecue; and Footloose.

Seven Cobra enemy sets made their debut: Alley-Viper; Targat; Heat-Viper; Frag-Viper; Night Viper; Annihilator; and Gnawgahyde with Wild Boar. The Cobra line expanded with the introduction of the Python Patrol. This series included six reissued action figures clad in new camouflaged outfits: Python-Officer, Viper, Tele-Viper, Crimson Guard, Copperhead, and Trooper.

A free face camouflage kit was enclosed in some GI Joe and Cobra figure packs. Each kit held tubes of white and black greasepaint.

Hasbro presented seven vehicles for the year's GI Joe line: the Crusader and Avenger (space shuttle and scout craft)with pilot Pay-Load; Thunderclap with Long-Range; Raider with Hot-Seat; Arctic Blast with Wind Chill; Mud-fighter with Dog-Fight; and Tri-Blaster with Radar Rat.

The Tiger Force vehicles acquired two vehicles: the re-outfitted Tiger Fish (power boat)and the Tiger Sting. Slaughter's Marauders offered the Armadillo, a one-man rocket tank; the Lynx, a cannon tank; and the Equalizer, an armored rocket launcher tank. The Battleforce 2000 vehicle roster expanded with the Pulverizer, a laser tank.

For the GI Joe Night Force line, Hasbro released a special "3-in-1" vehicle set, sold only through Toys "R" Us. These vehicles were the Night Scrambler, Night Ray, and Night Boomer,

BELOW: The Cobra Frag-Viper featured an enticing assortment of equipment.

RIGHT:
The name of the exotic TARGAT was an acronym for Transatmospheric Rapid Global Assault Trooper.

BELOW:
The package for Dreadnok Poacher, Gnawgahyde, included not only his pet wild boar, but a free command ring as well.

each offering glow-in-the-dark features.

Benny's, another retail chain, carried an exclusive GI Joe/Cobra set with two vehicles and four figures: the GI Joe Mudfighter bomber jet with pilot Mudfight; the Cobra HISS II troop transport tank driver Track-Viper; and two randomly selected figures.

Six Cobra vehicles introduced were: the Condor Z-25 jet fighter bomber with pilot Aero-Viper; the Razor Back with Wild Boar; the HISS II with Track-Viper; the Evader with Darklon; the Devastator; and a Hovercraft. Prices ranged from $2.59 to $20.49.

Cobra's Python Patrol series added three re-outfitted sets: the ASP gun emplacement; Stun split-attack vehicle; and the Conquest fighter jet.

GI Joe's visibility continued to increase on many fronts. On television a sixth cartoon mini-series (again in five parts) aired in September 1989, under the title *Operation Dragon Fire*. And in public relations Hasbro launched the second GI Joe "Search for Real American Heroes."

CHAPTER FIVE

GI Joe® in the 1990s

1990

Since the demise of the original-sized GI Joe, thousands of individuals, both young and old, collectors and non-collectors, called or wrote to Hasbro requesting the old Joe's return. People at the company occasionally discussed the possibility of bringing back the original GI Joe, but one major factor seemed to stand in the way: cost. (In fact, as far back as 1980, a team of Hasbro designers worked on Project Blast Off, a secret effort to bring back the original GI Joe.)

Seemingly, the only cost-efficient way to reproduce this figure was to use existing molds, but the original GI Joe molds had deteriorated and eventually been disposed of. The cost of building molds would be astronomical.

In 1990, Vinnie D'Alleva, GI Joe product manager, and Greg Berndtson, GI Joe design director, discussed the revival of the old GI Joe with renewed interest, wondering how he could be integrated into the modern GI Joe series. Because their job was to conceive and execute new ideas, D'Alleva and Berndtson approached management several times, attempting to re-ignite interest in the original Joe. Each time their proposal was dis-

ABOVE: Rampart was a new recruit in the ongoing battle against GI Joe's horde of enemies.

missed, but they refused to give up. By year's end they would begin to see the fruit of their efforts.

This year's GI Joe series action figures numbered ten: Captain Grid Iron; Topside; Sub-Zero; Ambush; Salvo; Free-Fall; Rampart; Stretcher; Bullhorn; and Pathfinder. Seven new Cobra figures were: Undertow; Night-Creeper; Rock-Viper; Laser-Viper; SAW-Viper; Metal-Head and Range-Viper. A new series joined this year's GI Joe line—Sky Patrol, an assortment of six air assault troopers: Altitude, Airborne, Drop-Zone, Static Line, Skydive, and Airwave. Sky Patrol figures came with a silver parachute. All figure packs sold for $2.55.

With certain figures Hasbro offered a free Command Ring as an incentive. The former Flag Points were now termed Combat Pay, again offering points usable for purchasing certain figures or equipment.

Four new vehicles were issued for GI Joe: the Retaliator, a claw-equipped bomber copter and driver Updraft; the Avalanche, a snow tank with driver Cold Front; the Hammerhead, a fast attack four-wheel drive vehicle; and the Mobile Battle Bunker, an armored tank. Cobra vehicles were: the Rage; the Hammerhead with Decimator; Hurricane with Vapor; the Dominator; the Dictator with Overlord; and the Piranha. Sky Patrol offered four vehicle sets: the Sky Havoc, Sky SHARC, Sky Raven, and Sky Hawk.

A large playset, the General, was offered this year. The mobile headquarters included a Locust Copter with pilot Major Storm for $44.99.

To continue GI Joe's television presence, a third *Real American Hero* cartoon series was aired in September, featuring episodes with titles such as "United We Stand" and "Biok."

After countless attempts to gain favor for a revival of the original GI Joe, D'Alleva and Berndtson finally were vindicated. Once the idea was given a green light, they found many other Hasbro employees who shared their

BELOW: Static Line, a demolitions expert, came with a working silvery parachute.

back the big GI Joe. It has baby boomer appeal, it has collector appeal, and most important, we tried to do it in such a way that it would have kid appeal. That's why we gave him the light-and-sound gun."

The basic GI Joe figure (3 -inch style) issued this year included eleven characters: Dusty and Sandstorm; Low-Light; Big Ben; General Hawk; Heavy Duty; Sci-Fi; Red Star; Grunt; Snake-Eyes; Tracker; and Mercer, an ex-Cobra officer. Seven new Cobra figures were Crimson Guard Immortal; Snow Serpent; Desert Scorpion; Red Star; Incinerator; BAT; and Cobra Commander. Basic figure packages sold for $2.60.

The Sonic and Super Sonic Fighters for both GI Joe and Cobra series also were introduced. Each fully posable action figure featured a plastic backpack with pulsating lights that, when activated by the push of a button, were accompanied by electronic battle sounds.The four GI Joe Sonic Fighters were Tunnel Rat, Law, Dial-Tone and Dodger.

The Super Sonic Fighters were Lt. Falcon, Zap, Rock 'n Roll, and Psych-Out.

For Cobra there were two Sonic Fighters, Lampreys and Viper. Cobra Super Sonic Fighters were Major Bludd and Road Pig. Both GI Joe and Cobra Sonic Fighters were priced at $4.99, while Super Sonic Fighters were $5.29.

Kellogg's got into the act this year by offering a GI Joe Lifeline figure as a mail-in premium. Wal-Mart marketed an exclusive package: the GI Joe Rapid Fire

LEFT:
Zap, a new Super Sonic Fighter, featured electronic battle sounds and light, as well as a free collector card.

LEFT:
A Sonic Fighter, Law carried four weapons: pistol, laser pistol, machine gun, and laser rifle.

with a video cassette, *Revenge of the Pharaohs*.

Hasbro's Eco Warriors also debuted this year, each posable environmental warrior featured "Color Change Battle Damage." Packaged with gear and a

RIGHT: Also featuring a free collector card, mercenary Major Bludd was equipped with the unique"sonic disruptor cannon".

weapon designed to shoot water, an Eco Warrior would change color if hit by water.

The three GI Joe Eco Warriors were Flint; Clean Sweep; and Ozone. The three Cobra Eco Warriors were Cesspool; Toxo-Viper; Toxo-Viper II; and Sludge Viper. Each basic figure packs was priced at $3.99.

Eight packages of GI Joe vehicles were offered: Badger; Attack Cruiser; Brawler; Battle Copter with Major Altitude; Battle Wagon with Air Commando Troopers; and Skymate, Cloudburst,

and Spirit with Tracker. For the Cobra line there were five sets: Paralyzer; Ice Sabre; Interrogator with pilot; Night Vulture; and Sky Creeper.

The GI Joe and Cobra Air Commandos sets created for this year featured five fully posable figures, each with an aerodynamic glider that could fly up to 40 feet with the figure attached. Each glider came armed with pivoting machine guns. A Battle Copters assortment for GI Joe and Cobra also was available for the same price of $5.99. These Battle Copters would fly with the pull of a rip cord.

Cobra Eco Warriors gained a vehicle called the Septic Tank. The tracked vehicle featured a rotating, water-firing cannon.

To capitalize on the GI Joe Duke's success, a kid-sized Electronic Battle Gear set also was created. Included in the set were a combat helmet, goggles, and a Sonic Fighter pistol that could emit eight electronic combat sounds.

GI Joe items manufactured by companies under license from Hasbro included the following:

- Do-It-Yourself room decorations by Priss Prints.
- Keel-Controlled 6½-foot streamer kite by Spectra Star Kites.
- Nintendo video game cartridge by Taxan.
- Hawk and Snake-Eyes hand-held LCD game by Micro Games of America.
- Official Trading Cards by Impel Marketing, Inc.
- Presto Magix Stick and Lift Adventure Set by Rose Art.
- Videotape, *Arise, Serpentor, Arise*, by Family Home Entertainment.
- Comic books by the Marvel Comics Group.

The fourth *GI Joe, a Real American Hero* cartoon series aired from October 1991 to January 1992 and included episodes as such "Infested Island" and "The Ballad of Metal Head."

This year Hasbro suspended its

BELOW: Eco-Warrior, Flint, changed color if hit by water. The package offered a chance to win a trip to Universal Studios.

RIGHT:
Cobra Eco-Warrior, Sludge-Viper, looked as sinister as his name sounded.

product rotation system. Popular products now would continue to be available.

1992

In January of this year, the Official GI Joe Collector's Club of America organized its first convention. Hosted by club president James DeSimone, in Burbank, California, the extravaganza attracted the attention of scores of hard-core GI Joe collectors and would-be enthusiasts. The show's major attraction was a 200-square foot GI Joe diorama featuring over 150 of the original fighting men engaged in a mock battle.

Two Hasbro representatives, Vinnie D'Alleva and Kurt Groen (a GI Joe designer) brought an animated mini-movie titled *The Ode to GI Joe*, produced by Gregg Grant. It depicted a boy's collection of GI Joes that would come to life when the boy left his room. At the conference D'Alleva and

RIGHT:
The Electronic Battle Gear set allowed a GI Joe fan to play the part of a favorite character, Duke.

ABOVE: GI Joe and the Cobra Enemy—the conflict rages on.

Groen also discussed their marketing plan for the early 1990s, and unveiled Hasbro's prototypes for a new GI Joe Collector's Series.

At the February 1992 Toy Fair, Hasbro unveiled its new GI Joe Hall of Fame to groups of perspective buyers from around the world. The new collector's series was touted, "GI Joe, the name American boys grow up with, is the name men always remember." The Hall of Fame GI Joes were collector versions of the 3¾ inch characters from the 1980s and 1990 series. Each would be a specially numbered edition. The Hall of Fame line was based on the concept of the original GI Joe of the 1960s, but intended to encompass the modern fighting forces of the 1990s.

The inaugural characters for the line were Duke, Cobra Commander, Stalker, and Snake-Eyes. Each Hall of Fame figure came with a complete battle dress uniform, head gear and boots, along with the "A Real American Hero" insignia with two dog tags on a chain. A figure was armed with the push-button activated, electronic light and sound weapon, and came packaged with a color-coded battle figure stand, the *Official Combat Manual*, and more.

The Cobra Commander had no battle scar, though Duke and Stalker each had a scar on his right cheek, while Snake-Eyes had a scar across his left eye. Duke was the only figure with blonde hair; each of the others came with black hair or a mask. Duke's face,

RIGHT:
The Hall of Fame Duke, patriot and defender of right.

BELOW:
A special GI Joe Club uniform set reveals painstaking attention to detail in design and manufacture.

This year's figures in the regular (3¾-inch) GI Joe and Cobra series were armed with spring-loaded weapons that could fire projectiles. There were eight different basic GI Joe figures: Duke; Wet-Suit; Road Block; Big Bear; General Flagg; Gung-Ho, Barricade; and Wild Bill, selling for $2.65. Two new talking figures were General Hawk and Stalker, selling for $5.99. A mail-order Steel Brigade figure was issued this year, in all new colors of green, blue and gold, for the price of $8.95.

The Cobra series gained

LEFT: Stalker is armed "to the teeth." Notice the small GI Joe logo stenciled onto his shirt.

BELOW: Snake-Eyes, of the Hall of Fame, displays his deadly wares.

for the Hall of Fame series, was different than the Target Stores edition. For the release of the Hall of Fame figures, an entirely new body mold was designed, giving these figures a more muscular body than the Target-only Duke that used the body from Maxie's Rob.

Kirk Bozigian noted, concerning the difference in face designs, "The plan was always to change the face, helping to establish Target's item as a true collectible. In my opinion, the Target Duke is more collectible than the other Dukes. As we go forward we'll probably do more of that type of customizing—different heads or slightly changed packaging."

RIGHT: Hasbro published this colorful booklet to give even more exposure to its popular GI Joe product line.

mail-order Cobra Ninja Viper also was available.

The GI Joe Drug Elimination Force (DEF) was also a new entry in 1992. These figures featured electronic "Battle-Flash" weapons that simulated the visual explosion of real weapons. Of the DEF figures, good guys were Bullet Proof, Mutt, Cutter and Shockwave, and bad guys were Evil Headman and his Headhunters. Each was priced at $3.99.

GI Joe vehicles for the year were the Barracuda, a torpedo-launching one-four figure sets: Destro, Flak-Viper, Firefly and Eel. Two new talking Cobra warriors were Cobra Commander and Overkill.

Ninja Force, masters of hand-to-hand combat, was a new marque Hasbro introduced this year. Clothed in classic Ninja attire, these GI Joe and Cobra Ninjas came with Ninja weapons and featured spring-powered martial arts maneuvers. The GI Joe Ninja Force included Storm Shadow, Dojo, Nunchuk and Tjbang. There were two Cobra Ninjas—Slice and Dice. Each figure sold for $2.65, the same as the basic figures. A

RIGHT: General Flagg was equipped with an armored catapult that actually could shoot small projectiles.

man submarine; the Patriot; Fort America; Sonic Desert Apache; and Storm Eagle. Cobra vehicle sets were the Rat, a one-man Hovercraft that fired two flak rotors; the Parasite; the Air Devil with Aerialist; and the Earthquake. The GI Joe Eco Warriors' vehicle was the Eco-Striker,and the Cobra model was the Toxo-Zombie Battle Copter.

A large playset for The Real American Hero series was the GI Joe Headquarters, a command center with electronic lights and sound. Its more than twenty working features included a maneuverable missile cannon, two missile launchers, a double-barreled bazooka, a searchlight, and battle sounds and sirens. It was priced at $39.99.

Another playset, the Eco-Warriors Toxo-Lab was produced for Cobra. The bi-level laboratory featured Color-Change Battle Damage as well as a working crane and water cannon, and other components.

Hasbro created a new battle figure collector's case for transporting GI Joe and Cobra figures and equipment. The black plastic case had large storage areas and a carrying handle.

A new kid-sized set was the Snake-Eyes Battle Gear Set. The package included a firing crossbow with three soft vinyl darts; a Ninja hood and face mask; Katana sword; two throwing stars; commando knife; and goggles. The set retailed for $13.99.

LEFT:
Stalker,packaged with a free collector card, could yell battle commands.

LEFT:
Storm Shadow, now part of the new Ninja Force, could fight with realistic Ninja action.

RIGHT: Bullet-Proof, of the new Drug Elimination Force, fired a missle launcher that emitted an electronic "battle flash."

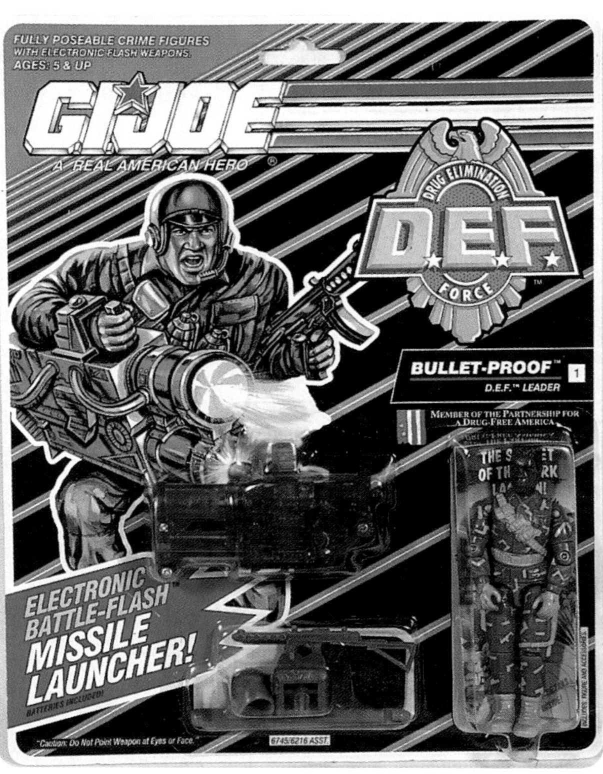

A video cassette from Family Home Entertainment was released in June. Titled *Revenge of Cobra*, it featured the five episodes in the TV syndication of 1986.

Hasbro GI Joe Trace-Plates also were introduced this year. The stencil set enabled kids to draw battle scenes with GI Joe and Cobra. They even could write dialogue in the voice balloons. The stencils for twelve GI Joe and Cobra characters, drawing paper, crayons, and pencils sold for $6.50.

For Christmas Hasbro shipped two new Hall of Fame figures, "Basic Training" Grunt and Heavy Duty. Rather than

RIGHT: With a Snake-Eyes Battle Gear set, a boy could wear a Ninja hood with face mask, and even fire the crossbow.

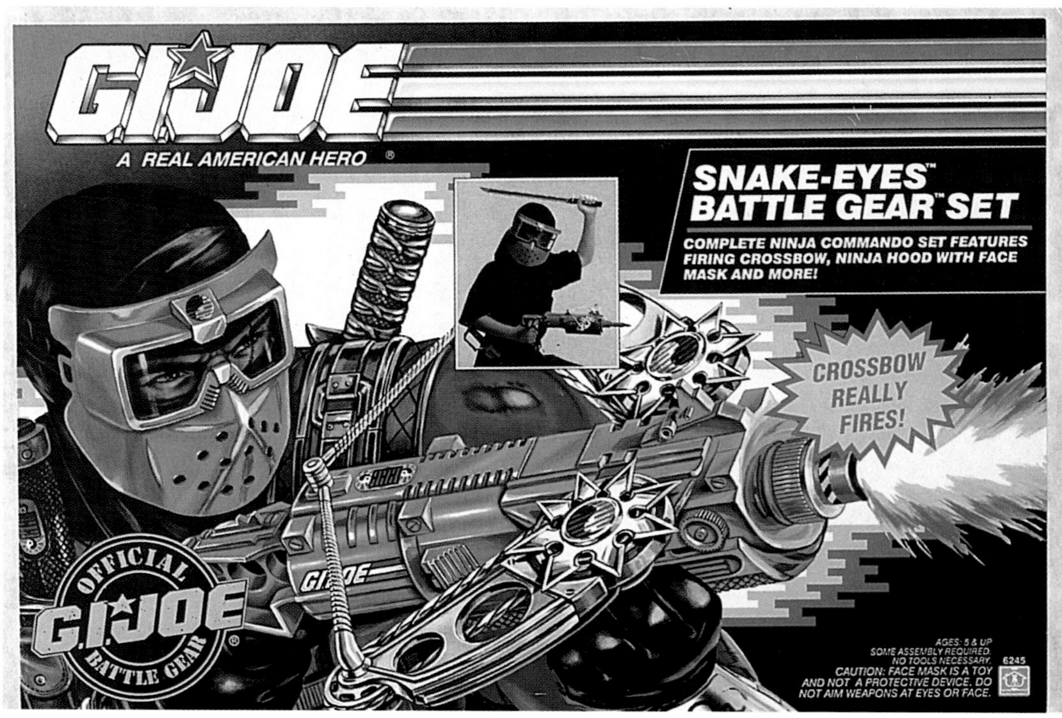

LEFT:
Grunt and Heavy-Duty show off the weapons they use in the fight against their relentless enemies.

the Sonic-Electronic weapons, they came with solid plastic weapons. The relatively small quantity of these collectors' editions, which went to major accounts such as Wal-Mart, Target and Toys "R" Us, sold out quickly at $12.99.

1993

Some of Hasbro's changes to GI Joe this year came as a result of new federal toy safety regulations, intended to protect consumers—especially small children. Toys now had to display appropriate warning labels, with text such as, "WARNING: Contains small parts that may present a choking hazard to children under three."

By the beginning of 1993, both Grunt and Heavy Duty had enjoyed a good sale and had received full distribution to toy retailers. Illustrated on the back of each Basic Training figure package were new Hall of Fame "Mission Gear" uniform and accessory sets (described later in this chapter), which first became available in February.

In addition to the depiction of Mission Gear sets, each box also carried a personality profile of the figure in the box, the profile to be clipped and saved for the collector's "Command Files." Each profile included the figure's code name, file name, serial number, primary military specialty, secondary military specialty, and birthplace, along with a complete biography, as well as a numbered listing of the set's contents.

Also pictured on the back of each new GI Joe box were the four original Hall of Fame fig-

RIGHT: Cobra Commander and Destro, of the Hall of Fame, model their fabulous arsenal and uniforms.

ures—Duke, Cobra Commander, Snake-Eyes and Stalker, each currently selling for $19.99. On the bottom of the box were four Flag Points and a GI Joe action figure proof of purchase, all to be used for mail-in premiums available from Hasbro.

In the wake of the first six Hall of Fame figures, Hasbro continued to release new models. To expand the Cobra line came Destro, wearing his distinctive "steel" mask. His armament included a spring-loaded machine gun with missile, and a knife and pistol.

At the 1993 Toy Fair, Hasbro displayed another Hall Of Fame figure package, Rapid Fire, the "Ultimate Commando." This would be a special limited edition set comprising nearly thirty accessories. In an exclusive arrangement with Toys "R" Us, Hasbro produced 100,000 of these specialty sets. Rapid Fire's accessories included such unique items as urban camouflage fatigues, and a micro-computer-equipped

LEFT: A close-up of Destro's famous mask.

backpack.

The fighter pilot Ace was another 1993 addition to the line. He came equipped with flight suit and oxygen mask. He also carried a combat knife, pistol, and combat rifle with missile launcher.

The former Cobra Viper, Storm Shadow, portrayed a Ninja master. With a "chameleon" camouflage hooded jacket, Ninja boots, and Katana sword, Storm Shadow made a unique addition to the Hall of Fame line.

Gung-Ho, the full-dress Marine, featured a shaved head with mustache, a USMC tatoo on his chest, and authentic dress blues. He was armed with sword and sheath, as well as combat pistol and assault rifle. As a model, Marine dress blues were borrowed from artist Kurt Groen's friend. However, to ensure that Gung-Ho's uniform was fully authentic, the designers sent a prototype of the figure to military history specialists at Quantico, Virginia. They returned it with a warning to undo the Fu-Manchu-style mustache. Marine regulations don't allow a mustache to extend beyond the corner of the mouth!

Each Hall of Fame figure was now packaged with with a spring-fired weapon, rather than a Sonic-Electronic weapon.

Duke made a second appearance as a 12-inch figure, this time as the talking Electronic Battle Command Duke. Equipped with a micro-processor that generated a voice for barking *thousands* of battle commands (with realistic sound effects), this Duke was armed with an automatic rifle and a spring-loaded missile launcher.

According to Hasbro's Kirk Bozigian, "The new Duke will be...much

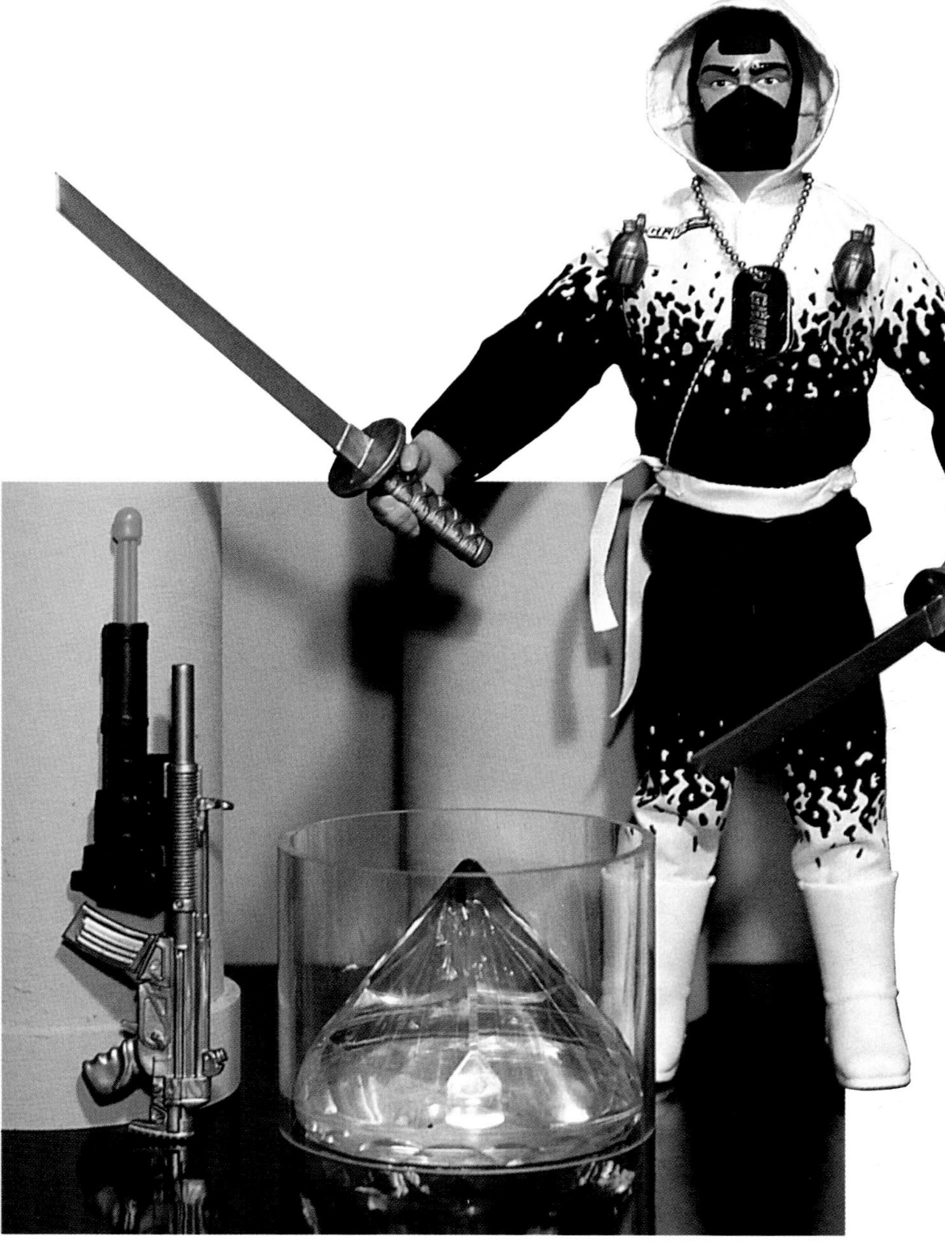

RIGHT:
With swords and automatic weapon, Storm Shadow stands ready to unleash his Ninja fury.

different from the old pull-string talkers. Now, upon the push of a button, the military figure can be activated to issue literally thousands of battle phrases, as well as realistic sound effects." The talking Duke was to retail for $39.99.

Vinnie D'Alleva said of these Hall of Fame figures, that "each GI Joe (and Cobra) character has been specially remodeled, but in the same likeness as the originals in the 1980s series." Each of these figures, of course, bore a consecutive serial number on its lower back.

Since the classic 12-inch Hall Of Fame Duke had arrived in 1991, GI Joe fans had hoped a vehicle soon would follow. Adult collectors who had grown up with Joe desired a four-wheel drive vehicle set reminiscent of the popular 1965 combat jeep.

In response to the demand for a vehicle, Hasbro's Dave Kunitz designed the Rhino GPV (General Purpose Vehicle), an all-terrain combat transport. The four-wheeled armored GPV measured almost two feet in length and one foot in height, scaled to hold four Hall of Fame fighting men.

With its oversized tires and massive bumper, the Rhino exuded an intimidating presence. It was armed with a large cannon that could launch up to eight plastic missiles with the flick of a switch. On the side of vehicle was a separate, M-60 sub-machine gun. The Rhino GPV retailed for $29.99.

Two large assortments of Hall of Fame "Mission Gear" uniform and equipment sets

LEFT:
The ultimate Marine, Gung-Ho proudly displays his Marine Corps tattoo.

RIGHT:
Hall of Fame figure, Flint, of the Army Special Forces, upholds the honor of the Green Beret.

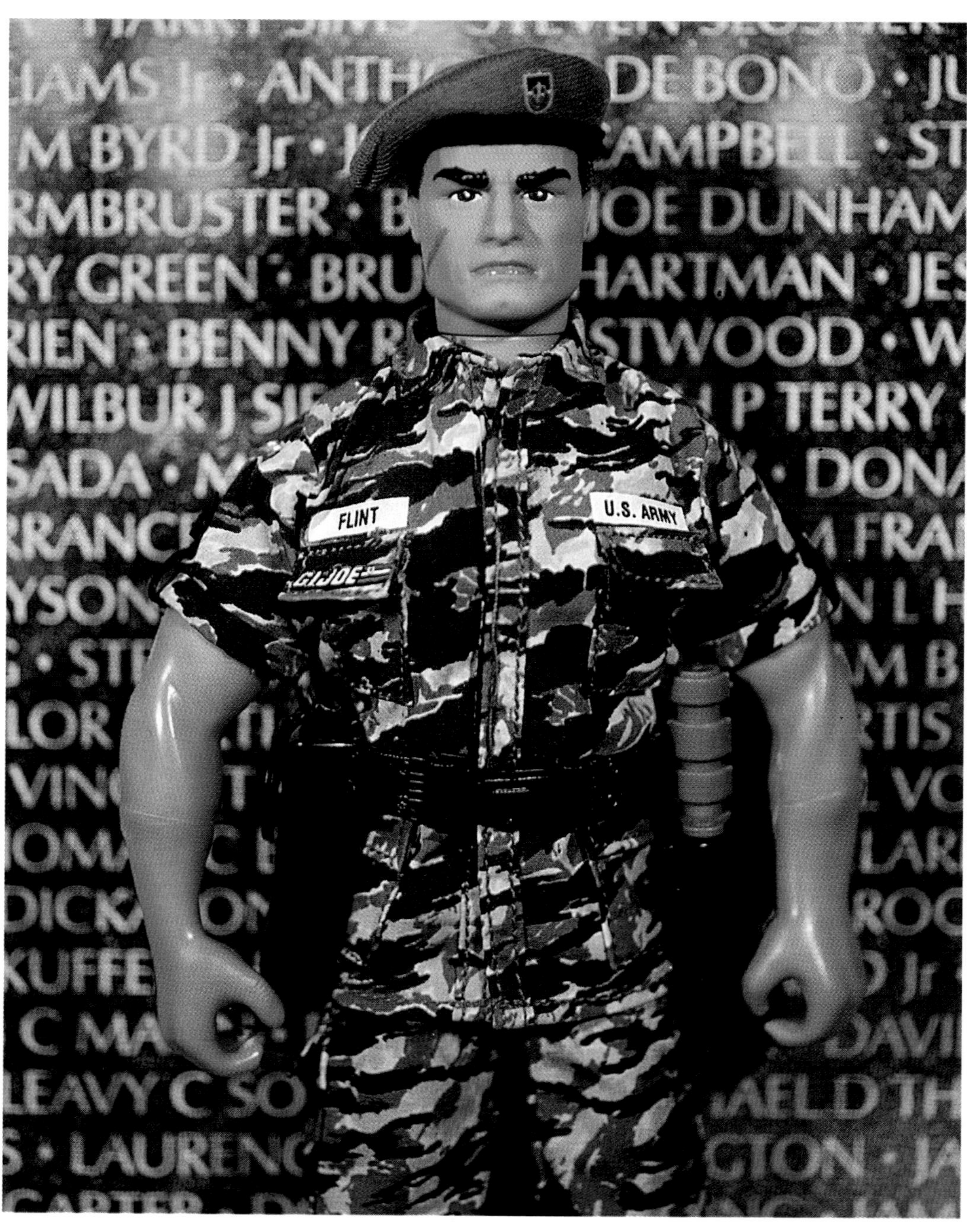

came on the market in 1993, the first being available in April, and the second in August. Each set contained a cloth uniform and gear, as well as a heavy artillery machine gun—with a spring-action launcher for firing miniature rocket missiles. Each set, packaged on a large blister card, retailed for about $7.

Mission Gear Assortment I items were: Arctic Assault, including parka, boots, skis, and ice crampons; Under-

water Attack, including scuba mask, suit and tanks, as well as a spear gun with scope; Light Infantry, including ammunition vest, T-bat propelling unit, and grappling hook launcher; and SWAT Assault, including military sweater with elbow patches, spotlight, and portable microcomputer.

Mission Gear Assortment II items were: Jungle Patrol, including Ranger Beret, assault vest, bandolier, pistol, knife, smoke grenades, and climbing rope; Desert Camo, including gog-

BELOW: Bristling with firepower, Rock 'n Roll defies his opponents with his menacing Gatling gun.

RIGHT:
With his lifelike hair and fine detail, and standing in this realistic set, the talking Duke looks as if he could come to life.

The four sets were: Army Boot Camp, including light infantry fatigues, baseball grenades, and AR-15 rifle with bayonet; Marine Parris Island, including grunts t-shirt and camouflage combat pants, AR-15 rifle with bayonet, and baseball grenades; Navy Shore Patrol, including special helmet, shirt and patrol pants, and pistol; Air Force Flyer, including flight suit, combat knife and M-16 rifle with bayonet.

By September, Hasbro Promotions and Direct had issued a full-color catalog to all subscribing members of Hasbro's Official GI

gles, combat watch, knife, grenades, and pistol; Red Ninja, including Red Ninja hooded shirt, knife, long sword, Katana sword, gas mask, climbing rope and grappling hook, and pistol; Mountain Assault, including cap and sweater, climbing crampons, goggles, rope and grappling hook and knife.

November of 1993 saw the introduction of Hall of Fame "Military Branch Outfits." These blister-packed sets, which included a cloth uniform and gear, as well as a firearm, retailed for $4.99 each. With each set came one U.P.C. Proof Of Purchase.

RIGHT:
The talking Duke stands tall in his unique display package. His electronic chip made him capable of speaking thousands of battle commands.

Joe Club. The catalog offered items such as 3¾ inch GI Joe and Cobra series figures, equipment, and vehicle sets, as well as offering special GI Joe Pocket Patrol figures, personalized action figures, a GI Joe Collectors kit with mystery action figure, and GI Joe sunglasses.

Of particular interest to the Hall Of Fame collector were two mail-order outfits with weapons for the 12-inch series. The GI Joe Infantry Outfit provided a "Fritz" styled combat helmet, short-sleeve infantry shirt and camouflage pants, pistol, and "Stinger" dagger.

The Cobra Infantry Outfit provided a shirt and pants, Luger pistol, and a Cobra "cutter" all-purpose knife. Each set cost $6.95 plus two Flag Points, or $8.45 without Flag Points.

September ushered in the Hall of Fame "Weapons Arsenals." Each set contained a unique weapon such as a

ABOVE: Hall of Fame's Rhino is everything a GI Joe combat vehicle should be. It features a fold-down windshield, shooting cannon, and M-60 machine gun, all complemented by rugged styling and mammoth tires.

grappling hook launcher or machine gun with spring-action missile launcher.

The Red Beret set featured a red beret, combat knife, baseball grenades, dagger, semi-automatic pistol, and assault rifle. The Green Beret set featured a green beret, M-16 missile-launching rifle, survival knife, Beretta pistol, and grenades. The Ultimate Arsenal set featured a Special Forces Ranger beret and helmet, machine gun, survival knife, baseball grenades, pistol, M-16 rifle with night scope, Ninja katana sword, combat diver's watch,and AR-15 assault rifle.

On an outing with his son and nephews, Hasbro's Kirk Bozigian noted their enthusiasm for a video game called "Street Fighter II." He recounted, "I looked at it, played it, and said, 'You know, this is a pretty interesting concept.' What they did was borrow everything from GI Joe. They created these characters, they ran these file cards and some of the characters looked like our GI Joe characters."

In 1993, under license from Capcom™, Hasbro launched a series of Hall of Fame figures under the name, Capcom™ Street Fighters II. The premiere set of 12-inch figures consisted of the video game characters with which kids were familiar.

The martial arts theme was a modest deviation, but Bozigian explained, "Well, we always tried to do GI Joe as a military concept.

What we're trying now to do is say that little boys can have many different

RIGHT: The Mountain Assault set provides a superb assortment of snow fighting gear, including snow camouflage parka, skis, and automatic rifle.

RIGHT: With an automatic weapon and survival knife to complement the orange jumpsuit, the Air Force Flyer has everything a Hall of Fame pilot needs.

adventures. We're never going to give up the military position because we own that, [and] that's what people know us for. But, who's to say that GI Joe couldn't have a superhero force? Or [be a] Capcom™ Street Fighter?"

Even though the Capcom™ Street Fighters were video-game characters,they still were very much in the GI Joe genre. Bozigian commented, "The idea is to make GI Joe appeal on different levels. So, if the kid isn't into military, maybe he's into this martial arts stuff. Maybe he's into Capcom™ Street Fighter as a video game. Maybe he'll want to buy into these characters. Maybe the kid who's not into the military, but into space, is going to buy our Star Brigade which is something else we've come out with. So, as we go forward, GI Joe is going to live in many different worlds."

In the 12-inch size series, four figures were introduced: Ryu, the Shotokan karate fighter; Guile, the Special Forces fighter; Blanka, the jungle native; and M.Bison, the grand master. These Hall Of Fame martial arts figures did not feature the trademark battle scar. Each did, however, come as a specially numbered collectors editions, packaged in a large window display box, and sported an au-

LEFT:
GI Joe's Navy Shore Patrol outfit, shown here with an inflatable raft, looks so realistic you almost can hear the ocean.

thentic battle uniform, a missile launching assault rifle, and other weapons and equipment.

The standard 3¾-inch series debuted with twelve figures: Ryu, Ken Masters, Guile, Chun-Li, Blanka, M. Bison, Edmond Honda, Dhalsim, Zangief, Vega, Balrog and Sagat. By August the products were in stores throughout the country, and selling better than expected.

Vehicle sets for the standard series included the Sonic Boom Tank with Guile; Crimson Cruiser with M. Bison; Beaster Blaster with Blanka and Chun Li. A Dragon Fortress playset (with Ken Masters and Ryu) featured a headquarters/training center with missile launcher, bungee platform, trampoline launcher, sparring target and more.

Ninja Force saw seven new figures, as well as vehicles such as Ninja Lightning, a motorized cycle; and the Pile Driver.

RIGHT: The Ultimate Arsenal is just what it claims to be. The set is like a soldier's superstore.

The year of 1993 seemed the beginning of new vigor for Hasbro's GI Joe line, for these were not the end of new GI Joe series. One of the new lines was labeled Battle Corps, and introduced GI Joe patriots, a gang of Cobra thugs. Each featured the swivel-arm battle grip. Vehicles for Battle Corps included Mudbuster, a 4x4 with missile launcher, grappling hook, and battering ram; and Ghoststriker X-19, an attack jet with engine and machine gun sounds.

Mega Marines were biotech fighters with moldable "bio-armor," made to fight genetically enhanced Mega Monsters. These figures also had spring-loaded features. A vehicle designed for this series was Monster Blaster APC. Sized to transport twenty Mega Marines, in included a spring-loaded missile cannon.

Star Brigade Armor Tech fighters featured futuristic robotic battle armor. Their vehicles included the Starfighter

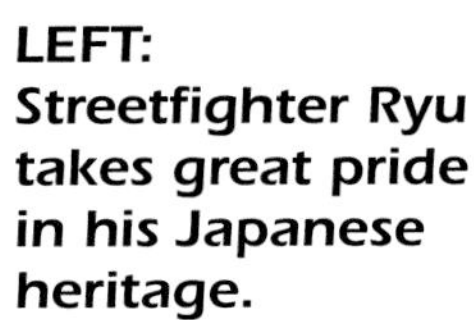

LEFT: Streetfighter Ryu takes great pride in his Japanese heritage.

LEFT: The bright, dynamic Street Fighter II logo, used by Hasbro under license from Capcom™.

RIGHT:
With his shock of orange hair and a bright blue body, Blanka is both intimidating and colorful.

FAR RIGHT:
Guile's tough-as-nails countenance is complemented by his combat knife, sword, and automatic weapon.

space jet, and the Invader, a one-man planetary attach vehicle with spring-loaded rocket launcher. The Star Brigade Armor-Bot was a robotic vehicle with electronic voice, lights, and sounds.

The Tonka division introduced a number of Steel Brigade military vehicles for GI Joe 3¾ inch figures. The four items were a 4x4 combat vehicle, pick-up truck, dump truck, and bulldozer.

A set of GI Joe trading cards appeared during 1993. In the first four Marvel comics GI Joe titles, a special trading card was inserted. The cards carried background information of GI Joe and Cobra, with pictures of them engaged in battle. The cards also featured collector tips for GI Joe enthusiasts.

When Hasbro released new figure series—Mega-Marines (Mega Monsters) and Star Brigade (Armor-Tech Star Brigade)—the maker inserted one of a series of twenty new cards with each figure. In order to get the complete set of twenty-four numbered cards, a collector had to purchase the first four editions of the Marvel GI Joe comic and the specified GI Joe and Cobra series figures. Each trading card carried an offer for a "free" GI Joe "Live Action Poster."

Hasbro's Kid Dimension division created a three-foot tall inflatable "Bop-Bag." Boasting "bounce back action" for indoor fun, the inflatable vinyl toy displayed full-color Capcom™ Street

Fighter II characters against which kids could test their skills—and unleash frustrations.

Other GI Joe products from Hasbro included the flying Zip-Cord Glider; a walkie-talkie set; a Kick 'em! Box 'em! action game; and a Ninja Force Power Bow that could shoot water or foam missiles.

Marvel Comics' *GI Joe* series of comic books had paralleled Hasbro's 3¾-inch action figure line since the introduction of the toy as *"A Real American Hero"* in 1982. In December of 1992, Hasbro launched its 1993 TV ad campaign, "World Of GI Joe," which spotlighted both the action figures and the comic book series.

For its key customers, Hasbro prepared a one-minute video that explained its new divide-and-

LEFT: Looking as if he had just stepped out of a science fiction drama, M. Bison stands proud and combat ready.

RIGHT: Marvel Comics' ***GI Joe,*** according to its creators, is "gritty" and "real," reflecting their intent to make it the definitive military comic.

RIGHT: GI Joe/Cobra trading cards featured photographs of actual GI Joe figures in action.

conquer strategy for GI Joe, including a glimpse of new GI Joe divisions: Battle Corps, Mega Marines, and Star Brigade. The entire line would be brought to life in upcoming issues of Marvel Comics.

Through the years the comic book series had chronicled the adventures

of GI Joe and Cobra, using a consistent, somewhat soft-core story line. That, however, was about to change.

Regarding the transition, former editor David Wohl said, "We want this book to become the definitive, contemporary military comic. We're allowing the book to become more gritty—more real. The [Hasbro] toy company wants us to be our own book. They know Marvel knows story telling, and so they trust us."

Wohl continued, "This new approach was more of an expansion of the current title, where familiar GI Joe characters would continue to be highlighted. The revamping enabled the book to reach its full potential, creating story lines which were as realistic as possible. On the average, we're going to have three to four-part story arcs."

The story arcs were to coincide with each of the new lines of GI Joe toys that Hasbro was producing. Wohl was careful to point out, however, that the comic book would not be directly influenced by the toy products. "While they reflect each other, they are different sides of the same coin," Wohl said.

Marvel comics writer Larry Hama, who has been working on the GI Joe comic exclusively since its debut in 1982, also writes the "Wolverine" and "Sabertooth" mini-series of the popular *X-Men* comic. Of the Hasbro/Marvel relationship, Hama observed that the company did not demand the book to be a certain way. "We're the final word on what happens with the book," he said. "Hasbro has been extremely

FAR LEFT: Cobranaut Astro Viper, a member of the new Star Brigade, attacked his foes with a shooting "astro-smasher."

LEFT: Gung-Ho, as a new Mega Marine, wore moldable "bio-armor."

open about it."

When Larry was asked about the "more real, more gritty" nature of the Joe comic series, he replied, "I don't write this as a kiddie book. I don't write *GI Joe* any differently from the way I write *Wolverine*."

The most popular character in GI Joe comic series is Snake-Eyes, so Marvel debuted a new "Snake-Eyes" sub-series. "Star Brigade" was a second sub-series launched in 1994. A fresh logo enhanced the new image of the comics series. The ad-laden GI Joe comic books offer the buyer thirty-two pages of full color for $1.25.

1994

No other action figure has undergone as many evolutionary changes as GI Joe—and yet endured for thirty years. And Hasbro's demonstrated commitment to the toy shows that the company expects GI Joe to be around for a long time.

The Hall Of Fame line, well-received by GI Joe fans of every age, already has become a hot collectible, with a strong, powerful look that appeals to kids. Ever since the first set of classic 12-inch figures debuted in 1992, the series has been aggressively marketed, with a deluge of television commercials nationwide—on all major networks, on spot TV and on Kid Cable.

Thanks to Hasbro's ongoing effort to evaluate and improve the classic 12-inch figure, in 1994, the Hall of Fame GI Joe will have more posability—without a major price increase. As the series progresses, Hasbro will introduce new characters but also update the original four figures by introducing new outfits and equipment, different packaging, etc.

As a response to collector enthusiasm, Hasbro will launch special limited edition figure sets. In early 1994 Hasbro began promoting the Lt. Joseph

RIGHT:
Rock 'n Roll is a spectacular comic book hero.

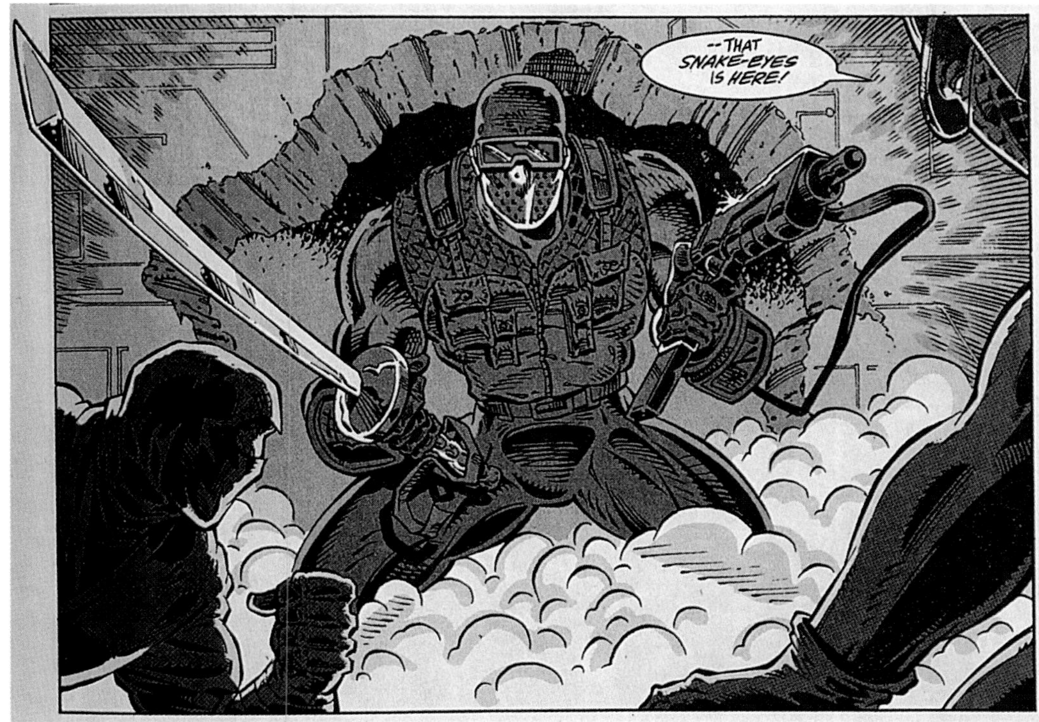

LEFT: Snake-Eyes is the most popular character in the comic book series.

Colton figure, dressed in Green Beret battle fatigues, and equipped with an automatic weapon and grenades; the figure is mounted on a wood base with an engraved plaque. The figure was available only through Hasbro Promotions & Direct, for twenty UPC Proofs of Purchase from GI Joe figures.

Other Hall of Fame figures will include new versions of Duke, Roadblock, Flint, Rock 'n Roll, Major Bludd, and Snake-Eyes. Vehicles will include a Strike Cycle and a Desert Rhino. An expected equipment set is the Battle Bunker.

Other series will continue to be launched, with colorful names such as Power Fighters and Manimals.

As for other coming developments, we can only guess. However, the recent dynamism of Hasbro's GI Joe product development holds promise for an exciting future.

The question of a major movie has been frequent among GI Joe enthusiasts. The fact that the action figure acquired his name from the 1945 movie makes a new film seem only fitting. A major development toward the possibility of a movie occured during GI Joe's 30th anniversary year. An article in *Variety* (Feb. 3, 1994) announced that Hasbro had discussed termswith producer Larry Kasanoff for a package of film and interactive projects. Former Hasbro president Larry Bernstein said of Kasanoff,

"We couldn't think of a better person to translate the legend of GI Joe into an exciting, unforgettable live-action feature film." Kasanoff's plans included a big-budget film; animated and live-action TV series; interactive video games; and even a possible theme park. As this book went to press, the future of these projects remained tentative.

RIGHT & FAR RIGHT: To commemorate GI Joe's thirtieth birthday, Hasbro has released a superb assortment of thirtieth anniversary figures. Here are Hasbro's own catalog displays of some of these figures, for both the Hall of Fame series, as well as the 3¾ inch line.

CHAPTER SIX

Creating GI Joe®

Enthusiasm is everything in designing new toys, and Hasbro's Dave DesForges is very enthusiastic about GI Joe. DesForges designs figures for Battle Corps, Ninja Force, Capcom™ Street Fighter II, Mega Marines/Mega Monsters, Star Brigade, and Armor Tech Star Brigade series.

With Hasbro since 1988, DesForges has designed packaging for the Transformers Robots, Conan the Adventurer, Monster Face and an assortment of other favorites. Today, he holds the position of Design Illustrator

BELOW: The creation of a new GI Joe figure first requires sketches of the artist's concept. Shown are samples from a number of such attempts. Art by Ron Rudat.

in the company's Research and Development Department.

When DesForges was growing up he had three of the original GI Joes. He remembers, "As a kid I liked the Action Marine the best because my dad was a Marine."

As a childhood GI Joe enthusiast, DesForges knows how important GI Joe has become to the ever-growing world of boys' action figures. He realizes the desirability that the figure needs for both the casual consumer and the hard core collector. He comments, "When I design GI Joe, I do it for kids—but I also understand that the figure must have collector appeal for adults."

LEFT: As a figure concept evolves, it is illustrated in a complete, detailed drawing—complete with color. This drawing depicts the figure Firefly.

The 3¾ inch line of GI Joe figures, designed by DesForges, supplies the foundation for 12-inch Hall of Fame figures. Any additions to that line begin after Hasbro's marketing people determine which are the best-selling characters. From there, the concepts for future 12-inch figures go through a complex process, with the cooperation of many highly talented individuals.

Kurt Groen, a senior design illustrator in Hasbro's art department, is the force behind the phenomenally successful GI Joe Hall of Fame series. Groen came to the company during February 1989—the month of GI Joe's twenty-fifth birthday. He has been designing the entire GI Joe series, including everything from the figures and their unique faces, to clothing and weaponry.

A graduate of the Joe Kubert School of Cartoon and Graphic Art and Design, Groen credits comic book artists as his childhood inspirations. Now he incorporates his own dynamic style and ideas into his characters, deciding whom they will look like, what they will be wearing, and with which weapons they will be equipped.

Aware of how many people ap-

RIGHT:
Art for the figure that eventually was named Roadblock

preciate his work, Groen acknowledges, "Creating GI Joe is a very gratifying job."

After Groen completes two-dimensional sketches, the drawings are developed by other parts of the company. In the sculpting department, for instance, Beth Buvarsky is responsible for producing an aesthetic, three-dimensional sculpture of a head out of Groen's sketches. "It's like a puzzle," Buvarsky comments. "What seemingly works on paper in 2-D might not at all work in sculpting, which is 3-D." She usually receives sketches about eight months before the figure's release date.

Buvarsky came to the company with excellent credentials, including a degree in metalsmithing and jewelry making. With a B.F.A. from the Rhode Island School Of Design, and an M.F.A. from the Rochester Institute of Technology, she acts as Project Director of Boys Toys Sculpture at Hasbro.

Buvarsky has so far created at least a half-dozen characters in the Hall of Fame, including Duke (1992), Grunt (1992), Ace (1993), and the Cobra: Destro (1992). Outside firms and freelance sculptors were responsible for creating the other Hall of Fame personalities.

Buvarsky's most gratifying sculpting project has been Grunt. For a model she used Hasbro employee, Steve Gibere, who sports a mean crew cut—and even looks a GI Joe. Gibere, admits Buvarsky, offered a unique challenge. "Steve has a very unusual face," she observes, "with interesting features."

In addition to sculpting these Hall of Fame figures, Beth also has had a hand in "fine-tuning" the facial features of heads submitted by outside contractors.

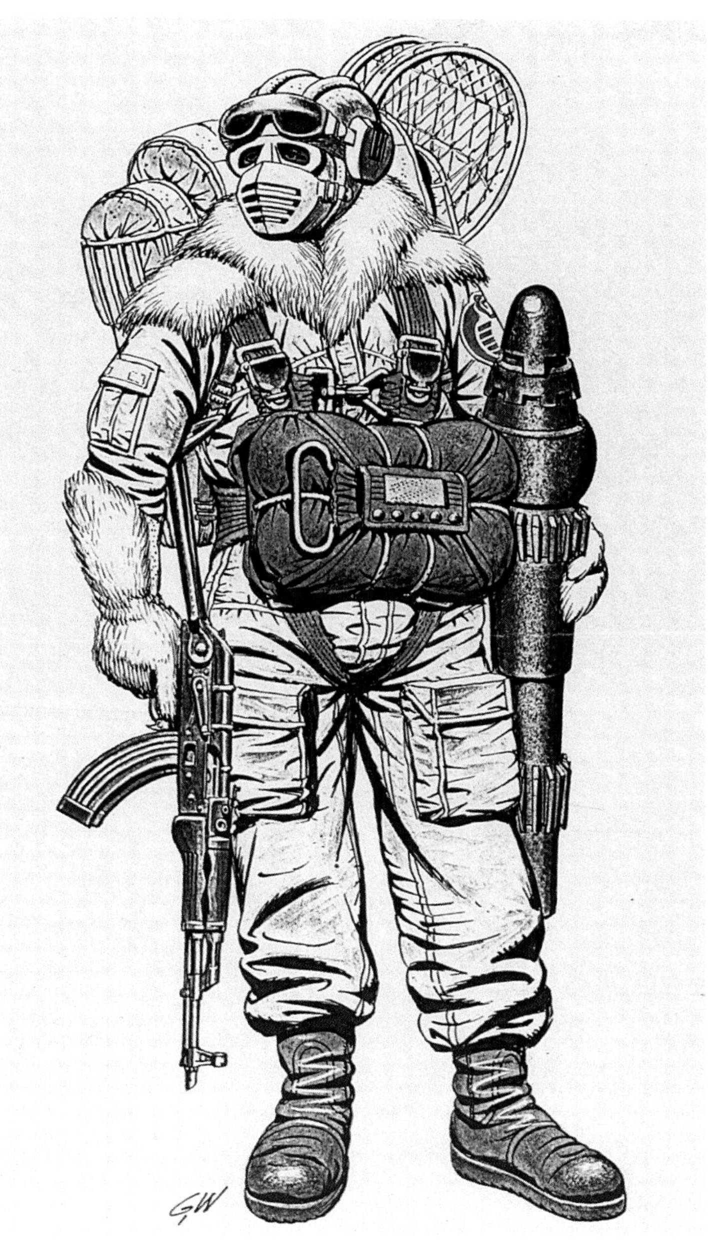

Before sculpting a head, Buvarsky plans for the head to be nine to eleven percent larger than final size—to compensate for shrinkage when it is electroplated in the mold-making process. She then begins with clay, a material which allows her to "work out all the problems: the look in the figures eyes, if the eyes are squinted, if the eyebrows are raised, the shape of the scar—almost everything. It's easier to work out problems in modeling clay rather than wax."

From the clay head a silicone outer mold is made. The clay head then is removed from the center, and liquid modeling wax is poured into the cavity. The wax replica allows a sculptor to add the subtleties, the fine details. With various instruments, Buvarsky tools the figure's features. She carves the ears; refines the nose; builds up the cheeks; and forms the jaw, chin and thickness of the neck. She then finishes the eyes, giving them the intimidating, GI Joe stare.

A few wrinkles give the face character, and then the lips complete the facial expression. The battle scar and eyebrows are the final touch.

After over fifty hours of work, the head is submitted for approval. At this point Vinnie D'Alleva, Kurt Groen, Kirk Bozigian, Greg Berndtson and Larry Bernstein give their okay and authorize the design for manufacturing, request modifications, or sometimes reject the entire design.

Kurt Groen's drawings of GI Joe uniforms are brought to life with the assistance of Alana Klingensmith, Senior Design Director of Soft Engineering. Klingensmith personally creates the clothing patterns for the Hall of Fame figures, as interpreted from Groen's original drawings.

Klingensmith, who originally designed clothes for Coleco's Cabbage Patch dolls, makes a variety of outfits for each 12-inch figure, each constructed with factory production in mind. She and Groen choose fabric with appropriate color, texture, and fit, then submit each outfit to a series of "wash 'n wear" tests to ensure the outfits meet federal toy guidelines.

The initial costuming ideas for the 1992 Hall of Fame line were concentrated on "futuristic fantasy." In 1993, the focus revolved more around "authentic realism," with military costuming patterned after Government issue designs, just as the original GI Joe outfits from the 1960s series.

Klingensmith, whose credentials include a B.F.A. in fashion design from the Endicott College, as well as studies at Massachusetts College of Art and the University of Syracuse, says she enjoys "basic military outfits" the most. Her greatest challenge has been "the Marine Dress outfit Kurt designed for Gung-Ho, because of all the intricate details to the uniform."

The creation of GI Joe weapons and equipment approximates the process used for the figures. Rick Rossi, who directs Hasbro's modeling department, overseeing a shopful of technicians who create the weapons and

package is worth more money than the same toy "unwrapped."

2. "Mint" condition, means a toy is unused and still in its original package.

3. When starting a GI Joe collection, use a collector's guide that lists, by year, each item made.

4. When collecting GI Joe toys, try to acquire three of each item: one to store, one to trade, and one for play.

5. Keep together all pieces and accessories that came with a GI Joe toy. Clip and save each bio-card.

6. Even if a GI Joe figure is not in its original package, it will have excellent value if accompanied by all its accessories and its bio-card.

7. A GI Joe driver-figure, that originally was packaged with a vehicle, is collectible alone if accompanied by its bio-card.

8. An extra premium item, included with a GI Joe toy, is collectible—especially if it is with its entire set.

9. A bent corner, or other damage, on a package reduces the value of a "mint" GI Joe toy. Store a toy *carefully.*

10. To display a GI Joe toy collection, try hanging figure cards on pegs, as stores do.

11. A GI Joe toy manufactured in limited quantity will have greater value than toys made in large quantities.

12. Certain GI Joe figures with "favorite" personalities and package art, as well as outstanding package art, are considered more valuable than others.

13. A variation in packaging, decoration, weaponry, or accessories, may increase the value of a GI Joe figure.

14. Develop a collecting strategy to make your GI Joe collection unique. Consider a focus such as year, theme, size, character, rank, or military branch.

15. Before buying, selling, or trading a GI Joe toy, use a collector's guide to verify its worth.

16. Keep a current inventory of your GI Joe collection, so you can know what you have and need.(This will be invaluable if you ever need to file an insurance claim.)

17. Join a GI Joe collector club to share information and make trades. If you can't find a club in your area, try to start one.

18. To prevent fading, protect your GI Joe toys from prolonged exposure to light—especially sunlight.

19. To maintain the condition of your GI Joe collection, store all items in sturdy, waterproof boxes, away from pets, dampness, and extreme heat.

GI Joe's Markings, 1964 Through 1976 -"The Original Years"

GI Joe's body had markings located on the right side of the buttocks, as listed below, that will aid you in dating the figure:

U.S.A.

GI JOE T.M.
COPYRIGHT 1964
by HASBRO ®
PATENT PENDING
MADE IN U.S.A.

Manufactured from 1964 through 1965. It showed that "GI Joe," the figure's name, was trademarked. Copyrighted in 1964 by Hasbro, the company's registered trademark. The figure's patent was pending. Body was made in United States.

GI JOE ®
COPYRIGHT 1964
by HASBRO ®
PATENT PENDING
MADE IN U.S.A.

Manufactured only in 1966. These markings were distinguished from the first issue of 1964-1965 by the absence of the letters "T.M." in the copyright notice. Now, the figure's name, "GI Joe," was a registered trademark. Copyrighted in 1964, by Hasbro, the patent Is still pending. Body was made in the United States.

GI JOE ®
COPYRIGHT 1964
by HASBRO ®
PAT. NO. 3,277,602
MADE IN U.S.A.

Manufactured from 1967 through 1975. "GI Joe" remains the registered trademark of the figure. Copyrighted in 1964 by Hasbro, the company's registered trademark. There was no problem distinguishing this 1967 version from the previous year's version. The patent was no longer pending, and a patent number was shown. Body was still made in the United States.

© 1975 HASBRO ®
PAT. PEND. PAWT. R.I.

Manufactured from 1975 through 1976. These unique markings were located on the bottom back torso of figures with lifelike bodies. Copyrighted in 1975, by Hasbro, the company's registered trademark. The patent was again pending. Body was made in the United States (at Hasbro's Pawtucket, Rhode Island factory).

CANADA

GI JOE REG T.M.
COPYRIGHT 1964
BY HASBRO ®
PATENT PENDING
MADE IN CANADA

Figures from the 1960s:

GI JOE REG T.M.
© RD 1964
HASSENFELD BROS, INC.
PATENTED 1966
MADE IN CANADA

Figures from the 1970s:
("MADE IN CANADA" was sometimes absent from markings)

GI Nurse Markings, 1967

PATENT PENDING
© 1967 BY HASBRO ®
MADE IN HONG KONG

The GI Nurse body had markings located on the lower back torso of the figure on every issue. Manufactured only in 1967. The GI Nurse had its patent pending. Copyrighted in 1967 by Hasbro, the company's registered trademark. The entire figure, with uniform, etc., was made in Hong Kong.

Place of Origin

Every GI Joe set - figure, uniform, equipment or vehicle - has its place of origin marked on the box. Hasbro had a factory in the United States and in Canada. Boxes carry the usual copyright notices plus the location where the item was packaged. Boxes were either printed "MADE IN U.S.A." or "MADE IN CANADA."

GI Joe's Markings, 1982 Through 1993 - "The Following Years"

The 3-3/4-inch GI Joe "A Real American Hero" series figures had markings located on both the lower back torso and inside left leg. Markings read as follows:

Lower Back:

MADE IN HONG KONG	(1982 through 1984 series)
or MADE IN CHINA	(1985 through 1993 series, with the exception of reissued figures from the 1982-1984 molds)

Inside Left Leg:

© 1982
HASBRO
(single-year series)

(Copyright dates increased as years progressed)

© 1982-1983
HASBRO
(split-year series)

The new 12-inch GI Joe "Hall Of Fame" series figures had markings located on the lower back torso. Copyright dates increased as years progressed. Markings read as follows:

© 1991 HASBRO, INC. PAWTUCKET, R.I. 02862 MADE IN CHINA	(Markings for "Target" Duke)
© 1992 HASBRO, INC. PAWTUCKET, R.I. 02862 MADE IN CHINA	(Markings for Duke [reissued], Snake Eyes, Cobra Commander, Stalker, Grunt and Heavy Duty)
© 1993 HASBRO, INC. PAWTUCKET, R.I. 02862 MADE IN CHINA	(Markings for Battle Command Duke, Flint, Rock'n Roll, Ace, Destro, Storm Shadow, Gung-Ho, etc.)

Foreign-Made GI Joes

During GI Joe's popularity during the 1960s and 1970s, foreign toy companies, under license from Hasbro, manufactured a similar 11-1/2-inch action figure series for their children's toy market. Like the original Hasbro versions, the figures and equipment in these foreign series consisted of the basic GI Joe type figure. Each came issued with a different uniform with equipment, and offered different vehicles. Each set depicted the armed services of the particular country where the item was manufactured. However, there were adversaries entered into each line of figures.

COMPANY	LOCATION	SERIES
1) Ceji	France	Group Action Joe
2) Estrela	Brazil	Falcon
3) Geyper	Spain	Geyper Man
4) Kenbrite	Australia	GI Joe
5) Toltoys	Australia	Action Man
6) Polistil Co. Ltd.	Italy	GI Joe Action Team
7) Politoy (Palitoy)	England	Action Man
8) Schildkrot	Germany	Action Team
9) Lily L.E.D.Y.	Mexico	Adventureos de Accion
10) Takara	Japan	Combat Joe
11) Vefi-Li	Argentina	Hombres D Action/ Comandos en Accion'

CHAPTER EIGHT

A Genealogy of GI Joe

Note: Each piece that came with a GI Joe set has been listed. If it is not listed, it did not come with the set.

CODE:

B - BOXED
C - CARDED
F - FOOTLOCKER
BG - BAG

ACTION SOLDIER SERIES 1964-1968

FIGURE SETS

YEAR/ ITEM #	DESCRIPTION	ORIGINAL PRICE	CODE
1964			
7500	Action Soldier	4	B
1965			
7900	Action Soldier (Black)	4	B
7531	Machine Gun Emplacement Set (Sears)	4.99	B
1966			
7536	Green Beret	8	B
5969	Forward Observer Set (Sears)	6.98	B
5978	Green Beret Machine Gun Outpost Set (Sears)	9.99	B
1967			
5904	Canadian Mountie Set (Sears/Simpsons)	7.98	B
7590	Talking Action Soldier	7	B
1968			
7549.83	Adventure Pack: Army Bivouac Series	10	B
7557.83	Talking Adventure Pack: Mountain Troops Series	10	B
90513	Talking Adventure Pack: And Bivouac Equipment	10	B
90517	Talking Adventure Pack: And Command Post Equipment	10	B
90532	Talking Adventure Pack: And Special Forces Equipment	10	B

VEHICLE SETS

YEAR/ ITEM #	DESCRIPTION	ORIGINAL PRICE	CODE
1965			
7000	Official Jeep Combat Set	15	B
7000	Official Jeep Combat Set with Moto-Rev sound	15	B
1967			
8030	Desert Patrol Attack Jeep Set and GI Joe Desert Fighter	11	B

VEHICLE SETS (IRWIN)

YEAR/ ITEM #	DESCRIPTION	ORIGINAL PRICE	CODE
1967			
5651	Motorcycle and Sidecar (14-inch)	3.39	B
5652*	Military Staff Car (24-1/2-inch)	5.99	B
5693	Amphibious Duck (26-inch)	4.67	B
5694	Personnel Carrier/Mine Sweeper (26-inch)	3.66	B
5395*	Helicopter (28-inch)	3.97	B
5396*	Jet Fighter Aeroplane (30-inch)	4.99	B
5397*	Armored Car (20-inch) (Friction-powered*)	4.67	B

UNIFORM SETS

YEAR/ ITEM #	DESCRIPTION	ORIGINAL PRICE	CODE
1964			
7521	Military Police Set	5	B
1965			
7531	Ski Patrol Set	5	B
1966			
7532	Special Forces Set	5	B
1967			
7537	West Point Cadet Set	5	B
7539	Military Police Set	4.50	B
1968			
7537	West Point Cadet Set (Reissued)	5	B
7539	Military Police Set (Reissued)	4.50	B

EQUIPMENT SETS

YEAR/ ITEM #	DESCRIPTION	ORIGINAL PRICE	CODE
1964			
7501	Combat Field Jacket Set	3.50	B
7502	Combat Field Pack (Reconnaissance Set)	3.50	B
7503	Combat Fatigue Shirt	1.20	C
7504	Combat Fatigue Pants	1	C
7505	Combat Field Jacket	1.80	C
7506	Combat Field Pack	2	C
7507	Combat Helmet Set	1	C
7508	Combat Sandbags Set	1	C
7509	Combat Mess Kit Set	1	C
7510	Combat Rifle Set	1.20	C
7511	Combat Camouflaged Netting Set	1	C
7512	Bivouac Sleeping Bag Set	3.50	B
7513	Bivouac Deluxe Pup Tent Set	4.50	B
7514	Bivouac Machine Gun Set	1.20	C
7515	Bivouac Sleeping Bag	1.40	C
7517	Command Post Poncho Set	4	B
7518	Command Post Small Arms Set	1	C
7519	Command Post Poncho	1.40	C
7520	Command Post Field Radio & Telephone Set	1.80	C
7523	M.P. Duffle Bag Set	1.20	C
7524	M.P. Ike Jacket Set	1.80	C
7525	M.P. Ike Pants Set	1	C
7526	M.P. Helmet and Small Arms Set	1.20	C
1965			
7527	Ski Patrol Helmet and Small Arms Set	1.80	C
1966			
7522	Jungle Fighter Set	1.60	C
7528	Special Forces Bazooka Set	1.60	C
7529	Snow Troops Set	1.40	C
7533	Green Beret and Small Arms Set	1.80	C
1967			
7510	Combat Rifle/Helmet Set	1.20	C
7514	Bivouac Machine Gun Set (Reissued)	1.20	C
7516	Sabotage Set	4.50	B
7520	Command Post Field Radio and Telephone Set (Reissued)	1.80	C
7522	Jungle Fighter (Reissued)	1.60	C
7526	M.P. Helmet and Small Arms Set (Reissued)	1.20	C
7527	Ski Patrol Helmet and Small Arms Set (Reissued)	1.80	C
7528	Special Forces Bazooka Set (Reissued)	1.60	C
7529	Snow Troops Set (Reissued)	1.40	C
7533	Green Beret and Small Arms Set (Reissued)	1.80	C
7538	Heavy Weapons Set	4.50	B
7571	Combat Engineer Set	1.80	C
7572	Combat Construction Set	1.40	C
7573	Combat Demolition Set	1.20	C
1968			
7516	Sabotage Set (Reissued)	4.50	B
7538	Heavy Weapons Set (Reissued)	4.50	C
7540	Combat Set	4	B

ACTION SAILOR SERIES 1964-1968

FIGURE SETS

YEAR/ ITEM #	DESCRIPTION	ORIGINAL PRICE	CODE
1964			
7600	Action Sailor	4	B
1967			
7690	Talking Action Sailor	7	B
1968			
7643.83	Adventure Pack: Navy Scuba Series 1,500	10	B
90612	Talking Adventure Pack: And Shore Patrol Equipment	10	B
90621	Talking Adventure Pack: And Landing Signal Officer Equipment	10	B

VEHICLE SETS

YEAR/ ITEM #	DESCRIPTION	ORIGINAL PRICE	CODE
1966			
8050	Official Sea Sled and Frogman Set	14	B
5979	Official Sea Sled and Frogman Set with Underwater Cave (Sears)	9.99	B
5979	(Same as above without GI Joe)	5.99	B

UNIFORM SETS

YEAR/ ITEM #	DESCRIPTION	ORIGINAL PRICE	CODE
1964			
7602	Navy Frogman Set	5	B
7612	Shore Patrol Set	4.50	B
1965			
7620	Deep Sea Diver Set	8	B
1966			
7621	Landing Signal Officer Set	4.50	B
1967			
7612	Shore Patrol Set	4.50	B
7623	Deep Freeze Set	5	B
7624	Annapolis Cadet Set	5	B
7625	Breeches Buoy Set	4.50	B
1968			
7602	Navy Frogman Set (Reissued)	5	B
7620	Deep Sea Diver Set (Reissued)	8	B
7623	Deep Freeze Set (Reissued)	5	B
7624	Annapolis Cadet Set (Reissued)	5	B
7625	Breeches Buoy Set (Reissued)	4.50	B

EQUIPMENT SETS

YEAR/ ITEM #	DESCRIPTION	ORIGINAL PRICE	CODE
1964			
7601	Sea Rescue Set	3	B
7603	Frogman Scuba Top Set	1.60	C
7604	Frogman Scuba Bottoms	1	C
7605	Frogman Scuba Equipment Set	1	C
7606	Frogman Scuba Tanks	1.20	C
7607	Navy Attack Set	3	B
7608	Navy Attack Work Shirt	1.20	C
7609	Navy Attack Work Pants	1	C
7610	Navy Attack Helmet Set	1	C
7611	Navy Attack Life Jacket	1.80	C
7613	Shore Patrol Dress Jumper Set	1.80	C
7614	Shore Patrol Dress Pants	1	C
7615	Shore Patrol Sea Bag	1.20	C
7616	Shore Patrol Helmet and Small Arms Set	1.20	C
1965			
7618	Navy Machine Gun Set	1.20	C
7619	Navy Dress Parade Rifle Set	1.20	C
1966			
7622	Sea Rescue Set (Reissued with life preserver)	4.50	B
7626	Navy L.S.O. Equipment Set	1.40	C
7627	Navy Life Ring	1	C
7628	Navy Basics Set	1	C

ACTION MARINE SERIES 1964-1968

FIGURE SETS

YEAR/ ITEM #	DESCRIPTION	ORIGINAL PRICE	CODE
1964			
7700	Action Marine	4	B
1967			
7790	Talking Action Marine	7	B
1968			
7733.83	Adventure Pack: Marine Medic Series	10	B
90711	Talking Adventure Pack: And Tent Set Equipment	10	B
90712	Talking Adventure Pack: And Field Pack Equipment	10	B

UNIFORM SETS

YEAR/ ITEM #	DESCRIPTION	ORIGINAL PRICE	CODE
1964			
7710	Dress Parade Set	5	B
1967			
7731	Tank Commander Set	5	B
7732	Jungle Fighter Set	5	B
1968			
7710	Dress Parade Set (Reissued)	5	B
7731	Tank Commander Set (Reissued)	5	B
7732	Jungle Fighter Set (Reissued)	5	B

EQUIPMENT SETS

YEAR/ ITEM #	DESCRIPTION	ORIGINAL PRICE	CODE
1964			
7701	Communications Poncho Set	4	B
7702	Communications Poncho	1.40	C
7703	Communications Field Set	1.80	C
7704	Communications Flags Set	1.60	C
7705	Paratrooper Parachute Pack Set	3.50	B
7706	Paratrooper Small Arms Set	1.60	C
7707	Paratrooper Helmet Set	1	C
7708	Paratrooper Camouflage Set	1	C
7709	Paratrooper Parachute Pack	2	C
7711	Beachhead Assault Tent Set	4.50	B
7712	Beachhead Field Pack Set	4	B
7713	Beachhead Field Pack	2	C
7714	Beachhead Fatigue Shirt	1.20	C
7715	Beachhead Field Pants	1.20	C
7716	Beachhead Mess Kit Set	1	C
7717	Beachhead Rifle Set	1.20	C
7718	Beachhead Flamethrower Set	1.20	C
1965			
7719	Marine Medic Set (with stretcher)	4	B
7720	Marine Medic Set	1.20	C
7721	Marine First Aid Set	1.80	C
1966			
7722	Marine Basics Set	1	C
7723	Marine Bunk Bed Set	1.40	C
7730	Marine Demolition Set	3.50	B
1967			
7703	Communications Field Radio and Telephone Set (Reissued)	1.80	C
7706	Paratrooper Small Arms Set (Reissued)	1.60	C
7717	Beachhead Rifle Set (Reissued)	1.20	C
7718	Beachhead Flamethrower Set (Reissued)	1.20	C
7720	Marine Medic Set (Reissued)	1.20	C
7723	Marine Bunk Bed Set (Reissued)	1.40	C
7725	Marine Mortar Set	1.80	C
7726	Marine Automatic Machine Gun Set	1.20	C
7727	Marine Weapons Rack Set	1.80	C
1968			
7730	Marine Demolition Set (Reissued)	3.50	B

ACTION PILOT SERIES 1964-1968

FIGURE SETS

YEAR/ ITEM #	DESCRIPTION	ORIGINAL PRICE	CODE
1964			
7800	Action Pilot	4	B
1967			
7890	Talking Action Pilot	7	B

VEHICLE SETS

YEAR/ ITEM #	DESCRIPTION	ORIGINAL PRICE	CODE
1966			
8020	Official Space Capsule Set and Authentic Space Suit	7.99	B
5979 Sears	Official Space Capsule Set (same as above with flotation collar, life raft & oar)	9.99	B
1967			
8040	Crash Crew Fire Truck Set and Silver Fire Fighter Suit	16	B

UNIFORM SETS

YEAR/ ITEM #	DESCRIPTION	ORIGINAL PRICE	CODE
1964			
7803	Dress Uniform Set	4.50	B
7807	Scramble Set	4	B
1966			
7820	Crash Crew Set	5	B
1967			
7822	Air Academy Cadet Set	5	B
7823	Fighter Pilot Set	8	B
7824	Astronaut Set	7	B
7825	Air/Sea Rescue Set	5	B
1968			
7822	Air Academy Cadet Set (Reissued)	5	B
7823	Fighter Pilot Set (Reissued)	8	B
7824	Astronaut Set (Reissued)	7	B
7825	Air/Sea Rescue Set (Reissued)	5	B

EQUIPMENT SETS

YEAR/ ITEM #	DESCRIPTION	ORIGINAL PRICE	CODE
1964			
7801	Survival Life Raft Set	3.25	B
7802	Survival Life Raft	2	C
7804	Dress Uniform Jacket Set	1.80	C
7805	Dress Uniform Pants	1	C
7806	Dress Uniform Shirt & Equipt. Set	1.60	C
7808	Scramble Flight Suit	2.25	C
7809	Scramble Air Vest & Equipt. Set	1	C
7810	Scramble Crash Helmet	1.20	C
7811	Scramble Parachute Pack	2	C
1965			
7812	Scramble Communications Set	1.80	C
7813	Air Force Police Set	1.60	C
1966			
7814	Air Force Basics Set	1	C
1967			
7808	Scramble Flight Suit (Reissued)	2.25	C
7809	Scramble Air Vest & Equipt. Set (Reissued)	1	C
7810	Scramble Crash Helmet (Reissued)	1.20	C
7812	Scramble Communications Set (Reissued)	1.80	C

YEAR/ ITEM #	DESCRIPTION	ORIGINAL PRICE	CODE
7813	Air Force Police Set (Reissued)	1.60	C
7814	Air Force Basics Set (Reissued)	1	C
7815	Air Force Security Set	1.60	C
7816	Air Force Mae West Air Vest & Equipment Set	1.40	C

GI JOE ACTION SERIES
1965-1968
ARMY, NAVY, MARINE AND AIR FORCE EQUIPMENT SETS

Footlockers

YEAR/ ITEM #	DESCRIPTION	ORIGINAL PRICE	CODE
1965			
8000	Basic Footlocker	4	F
1968			
8000.83	Footlocker Adventure Pack: with 16 items	7.99	F
8001.83	Footlocker Adventure Pack: with 15 items	7.99	F
8002.83	Footlocker Adventure Pack: with 22 items	7.99	F
1969			
8000.83	Footlocker Adventure Pack: with 16 items	7.99	F
8001.83	Footlocker Adventure Pack: with 15 items	7.99	F
8002.83	Footlocker Adventure Pack: with 15 items	7.99	F

EQUIPMENT SETS
4 SERVICES IN 1 SPECIAL

YEAR/ ITEM #	DESCRIPTION	ORIGINAL PRICE	CODE
1968			
8005.83	Adventure Pack: with 12 items	4.50	B
8006.83	Adventure Pack: with 14 items	4.50	B
8007.83	Adventure Pack: with 16 items	4.50	B
8008.83	Adventure Pack: with 14 items	4.50	B

UNIFORM SETS

YEAR/ ITEM #	DESCRIPTION	ORIGINAL PRICE	CODE
1968			
8009.83	Adventure Pack: with 37 items (dress parade)	6.50	B

ACTION SOLDIERS OF THE WORLD SERIES
1966-1968

FIGURE SETS
(Deluxe Sets with Equipment)

YEAR/ ITEM #	DESCRIPTION	ORIGINAL PRICE	CODE
1966			
8100	German Soldier	8	B
8101	Japanese Imperial Soldier	8	B
8102	Russian Infantryman	8	B
8103	French Resistance Fighter	8	B
8104	British Commando	8	B
8105	Australian Jungle Fighter	8	B
	(Standard Sets)		
8200	German Soldier	5	B
8201	Japanese Imperial Soldier	5	B
8202	Russian Infantryman	5	B
8203	French Resistance Fighter	5	B
8204	British Commando	5	B
8205	Australian Jungle Fighter	5	B
1968			
8111.83	Talking Adventure Pack: Foreign Soldiers of the World	10	B

EQUIPMENT SETS

YEAR/ ITEM #	DESCRIPTION	ORIGINAL PRICE	CODE
1966			
8300	German Soldier Set	2.79	C
8301	Japanese Imperial Soldier Set	2.79	C
8302	Russian Infantryman Set	2.79	C
8303	French Resistance Fighter Set	2.79	C
3304	British Commando Set	2.79	C
8305	Australian Jungle Fighter Set	2.79	C
1967			
Sears	Uniforms of 6 Nations	9.99	B

GI NURSE
ACTION GIRL SERIES
1967

FIGURE SETS

YEAR/ ITEM #	DESCRIPTION	ORIGINAL PRICE	CODE
8060	Action GI Nurse	8	B

THE ADVENTURES OF GI JOE SERIES
1969

FIGURE SETS

YEAR/ ITEM #	DESCRIPTION	ORIGINAL PRICE	CODE
1969			
7905	Adventurer	4.99	B
7905	Negro Adventurer	4.99	B
7910	Aquanaut	4.99	B
7915	Talking Astronaut	5.99	B

VEHICLE SETS
(Super Deluxe Sets)

YEAR/ ITEM #	DESCRIPTION	ORIGINAL PRICE	CODE
1969			
7980	Shark's Surprise Set with Frogman	10.99	B
7980.83	Shark's Surprise Set without Frogman (Reissued)	8.99	B
7981	Spacewalk Mystery Set with Spaceman	10.99	B
7981.83	Spacewalk Mystery Set without Spaceman (Reissued)	8.99	B
7982	Fight for Survival Set with Polar Explorer	10.99	B
7982.83	Fight for Survival Set without Polar Explorer	8.99	B

UNIFORM/EQUIPMENT SETS
(Basic Sets)

YEAR/ ITEM #	DESCRIPTION	ORIGINAL PRICE	CODE
1969			
7920	Danger of the Depths Set \ Aquanaut	6.99	B
7921	Mysterious Explosion Set \ Firefighter	6.99	B
7922	Secret Mission to Spy Island Set \ Secret Agent	6.99	B
7923	Perilous Rescue Set \ Rescue Diver	6.99	B
	(Deluxe Sets)		
7950	The Eight Ropes of Danger Set \ Underwater Diver	7.99	B
7951	The Fantastic Freefall Set \ Test Pilot	7.99	B
7952	The Hidden Missile Discovery Set \ Spaceman	7.99	B
7953	The Mouth of Doom Set \ Jungle Explorer	7.99	B

EQUIPMENT SETS
(Footlockers)

YEAR/ ITEM #	DESCRIPTION	ORIGINAL PRICE	CODE
7940	Adventure Locker	6.99	F
7941	Aqua Locker	6.99	F
7942	Astro Locker	6.99	F

ADVENTURE TEAM SERIES
1970-1973

FIGURE SETS

YEAR/ ITEM #	DESCRIPTION	ORIGINAL PRICE	CODE
1970			
7401	Land Adventurer	5.99	B
7402	Sea Adventurer	5.99	B
7403	Air Adventurer	5.99	B
7404	Adventurer (Black)	5.99	B
7500	Man of Action	5.99	B
7400	Talking Adventure Team Commander	7.99	B
7405	Talking Astronaut	7.99	B
7590	Talking Man of Action	7.99	B
1973			
7406	Talking Adventure Team Commander (Black)	8.99	B

VEHICLE SETS

YEAR/ ITEM #	DESCRIPTION	ORIGINAL PRICE	CODE
1970			
7005	Adventure Team Vehicle Set	8.99	B
7010	Space-A-Matic Set	8.99	B
7441	Secret of the Mummy's Tomb Set with Land Adventurer	8.99	B
7442	The Shark's Surprise Set with Sea Adventurer	8.99	B
7445	Spacewalk Mystery Set with Astronaut	8.99	B
1971			
7418	Search for the Stolen Idol Set	8.99	B
79-59092 Sears	Recovery of the Lost Mummy Adventure Set	17.99	B
1972			
7499	Mobile Support Vehicle Set	16.99	B
1973			
7380	Helicopter Set	6.99	B
	(IRWIN VEHICLES)		
23528-Sears	All-Terrain Vehicle (14-inch)	4.33	B
59114-Sears	Chopper Cycle (15-inch)	4.99	B
59158-Sears	Amphicat (13-inch)	4.99	B
59189-Sears	Giant Air-Sea Helicopter (28-inch)	8.99	B
59751-Sears	Combat Action Jeep (18-inch)	4.99	B

YEAR/ ITEM #	DESCRIPTION	ORIGINAL PRICE	CODE
J.C. Penney	Helicopter (14-inch)	5.99	B
J.C. Penney	Signal All-Terrain Vehicle (12-inch)	5.99	B
J.C. Penney	Action Sea Sled (13-inch)	5.99	B

UNIFORM/EQUIPMENT SETS

YEAR/ ITEM #	DESCRIPTION	ORIGINAL PRICE	CODE
1970			
7411	Secret Mission to Spy Island Set	3.99	B
7412	Danger of the Depths Set	3.99	B
7415	Hidden Missile Discovery Set	3.99	B
7422	Eight Ropes of Danger Set	4.99	B
7423	Fantastic Freefall Set	4.99	B
7425	Flying Space Adventure Set	4.99	B
7431	Fight for Survival Set	5.25	B
7436	White Tiger Hunt Set	5.25	B
7437	Capture of the Pygmy Gorilla Set	5.25	B
1971			
7340	Missile Recovery Set	3.99	C/B
7341	Radiation Detection Set	3.99	C/B
7342	High Voltage Escape Set	3.99	C/B
7343	Hurricane Spotter Set	3.99	C/B
7344	Volcano Jumper Set	3.99	C/B
7345	Aerial Reconnaissance Set	3.99	C/B
7370	Demolition Set	3.99	C/B
7371	Smoke Jumper Set	3.99	C/B
7372	Karate Set	3.99	C/B
7373	Jungle Survival Set	3.99	C/B
7374	Emergency Rescue Set	3.99	C/B
7375	Secret Agent Set	3.99	C/B
1973			
Asst. 7308-1	Hidden Treasure Set	2.75	C/B
Asst. 7308-2	Fight for Survival Set	2.75	C/B
Asst. 7308-3	Copter Rescue Set	2.75	C/B
Asst. 7308-4	Secret Rendezvous Set	2.75	C/B
Asst. 7308-5	Dangerous Mission Set	2.75	C/B
Asst. 7308-6	Desert Survival Set	2.75	C/B
Asst. 7309-1	Secret Mission Set	2.75	C/B
Asst. 7309-2	Dangerous Climb Set	2.75	C/B
Asst. 7309-3	Jungle Ordeal Set	2.75	C/B
Asst. 7309-4	Photo Reconnaissance Set	2.75	C/B
Asst. 7309-4	Winter Rescue Set (Replaced Photo Reconnaissance Set)	2.75	C/B
Asst. 7309-5	Desert Explorer Set	2.75	C/B
Asst. 7309-6	Undercover Agent Set	2.75	C/B
7439.16-Sears	Search for the Abominable Snowman Set	6.99	B
Sears	Mystery of the Boiling Lagoon Set	6.99	B

EQUIPMENT SETS

YEAR/ ITEM #	DESCRIPTION	ORIGINAL PRICE	CODE
1971			
7350	Rescue Raft Set	3.25	B
7351	Fire Fighter Set	3.25	B
7352	Life-Line Catapult Set	3.25	B
7353	Windboat Set	3.25	B
7354	Underwater Explorer set	3.25	B
7360	Escape Car Set	3.25	B
7361	Flying Rescue Set	3.25	B
7362	Signal Flasher Set	3.25	B
7363	Turbo Copter Set	3.25	B
7364	Drag Bike Set	3.25	B
7480	3 in 1 Super Adventure Set: Danger of the Depths, Secret Mission to Spy Island and Flying Space Adventure	17.99	B
7480	3 in 1 Super Adventure Set: Cold of the Arctic, Heat of the Desert and Danger of the Jungle	17.99	B
1972			
7310	Underwater Demolition Set	2.75	C
7311	Laser Rescue Set	2.75	C
7312	Sonic Rock Blaster Set	2.75	C
7313	Chest Winch Set	2.75	C
7314	Solar Communicator Set	2.75	C
7315	Rocket Pack Set	2.75	C
Asst. 7319-1	Escape Slide Set	2.75	C
Asst. 7319-2	Magnetic Flaw Detector Set	2.75	C
Asst. 7319-3	Sample Analyzer Set	2.75	C
Asst. 7319-4	Thermal Terrain Scanner Set	2.75	C
Asst. 7319-5	Equipment Tester Set	2.75	C
Asst. 7319-6	Seismograph Set	2.75	C

ADVENTURE TEAM PLAYSETS

YEAR/ ITEM #	DESCRIPTION	ORIGINAL PRICE	CODE
1972			
7490	Adventure Team Headquarters Set	14.99	B
1973			
7495	Adventure Team Training Center Set	14.99	B

ADVENTURE TEAM WITH KUNG-FU GRIP AND LIFELIKE BODY 1974-1976 FIGURE SETS

YEAR/ ITEM #	DESCRIPTION	ORIGINAL PRICE	CODE
1974			
7280	Land Adventurer	3.99	B
7281	Sea Adventurer	3.99	B
7282	Air Adventurer	3.99	B
7283	Adventurer (Black)	3.99	B
7284	Man of Action	3.99	B
7290	Talking Adventure Team Commander	4.99	B
7291	Talking Adventure Team Commander (Black)	4.99	B
7292	Talking Man of Action	4.99	B
1975			
8025	Mike Powers/Atomic Man	3.99	C

LIFELIKE GI JOE

YEAR/ ITEM #	DESCRIPTION	ORIGINAL PRICE	CODE
1976			
7270	Land Adventurer	4.99	C
7271	Sea Adventurer	4.99	C
7272	Air Adventurer	4.99	C
7273	Black Adventurer	4.99	C
7274	Man of Action	4.99	C
7276	Eagle Eye Land Commander	4.99	C
7277	Eagle Eye Man of Action	4.99	C
7278	Eye Commando (Black)	4.99	C
7280*	Land Adventurer	4.99	C
7281*	Sea Adventurer	4.99	C
7282*	Air Adventurer	4.99	C
7283*	Black Adventurer	4.99	C
7284*	Man of Action	4.99	C
7290*	Talking Commander	5.99	B
7291*	Talking Commander (Black)	5.99	B
7292*	Talking Man of Action	5.99	B
8026	Bulletman	4.99	C
8050	The Intruder Commander	4.99	B
8050	The Intruder Commander	4.99	C
8051	The Intruder Warrior	4.99	B
8051	The Intruder Warrior	4.99	C

*Deluxe Sets with Equipment

VEHICLE SETS

YEAR/ ITEM #	DESCRIPTION	ORIGINAL PRICE	CODE
1974			
7439	Devil of the Deep	7.99	B
7450	Fate of the Troubleshooter	11.99	B
7493	Sandstorm Survival Adventure	12.99	B
79-59301 (Sears)	Trapped in the Coils of Doom	13.99	B
1975			
7460	Fantastic Sea Wolf Submarine	9.99	B
7470	Sky Hawk	8.99	B
1976			
7000	Combat Jeep and Trailer	9.99	B
7380	Helicopter	5.99	B
7494	Big Trapper Adventure with Intruder	15.99	B
7498	Big Trapper (no figure)	13.99	B
7480	Capture Copter (no figure)	13.99	B
7481	Capture Copter Adventure with Intruder	15.99	B
Sears	Avenger Pursuit Craft	13.99	B

UNIFORM/EQUIPMENT SETS (Super Deluxe Sets)

YEAR/ ITEM #	DESCRIPTION	ORIGINAL PRICE	CODE
1975			
7413	Revenge of the Spy Shark	4.99	B
7414	Black Widow Rendezvous	4.99	B
7416	Peril of the Raging Inferno	4.99	B
7420	Attack at Vulture Falls	4.99	B
7421	Jaws of Death	4.99	B
7440	Sky Dive to Danger	6.99	B
Sears 59289	Trouble at Vulture Pass	5.99	B

(Deluxe Sets)

YEAR/ ITEM #	DESCRIPTION	ORIGINAL PRICE	CODE
Asst. 7328-1	Secret Courier	1.99	C
Asst. 7328-2	Thrust into Danger	1.99	C
Asst. 7328-3	Long Range Recon	1.99	C
Asst. 7328-4	Green Danger	1.99	C
Asst. 7328-5	Buried Bounty	1.99	C
Asst. 7328-6	Divers Distress	1.99	C
Asst. 7338-1	Danger Ray Detection	3.99	B
Asst. 7338-2	Night Surveillance	3.99	B
Asst. 7338-3	Shocking Escape	3.99	B
Asst. 7339-1	Raging River Dam Up	3.99	B
Asst. 7339-2	Jettison to Safety	3.99	B
Asst. 7339-3	Mine Shaft Breakout	3.99	B
Asst. 8028-1	Race for Recovery	1.99	C
Asst. 8028-2	Fangs of the Cobra	1.99	C
Asst. 8028-3	Special Assignment	1.99	C
8030	Secret Mission	4.99	B
8031	Dive to Danger	4.99	B
8032	Challenge of Savage River	4.99	B
8033	Command Para Drop	4.99	B

PLAYSETS

YEAR/ ITEM #	DESCRIPTION	ORIGINAL PRICE	CODE
8040	Secret Mountain Outpost	6.99	B

EQUIPMENT SETS

YEAR/ ITEM #	DESCRIPTION	ORIGINAL PRICE	CODE
1974			
7310	Underwater Demolition Set (Reissued)	2.75	C
7311	Laser Rescue Set (Reissued)	2.75	C
7312	Sonic Rock Blaster Set (Reissued)	2.75	C
7313	Chest Winch Set (Reissued)	2.75	C
7314	Solar Communicator Set (Reissued)	2.75	C
7315	Rocket Pack Set (Reissued)	2.75	C
8000	Footlocker (Reissued)	5.99	F

SUPER JOE 1977

FIGURE SETS

YEAR/ ITEM #	DESCRIPTION	ORIGINAL PRICE	CODE
1977			
7501	Super Joe Commander	3.60	C
7503	Super Joe	2.80	C
7504	Super Joe (Black)	2.80	C
7505	The Shield	3.60	C
7506	Luminos	3.60	C
7510	Gor	3.60	C
1978			
	Darkon	3.60	C
	Terron	3.60	C

UNIFORM/EQUIPMENT

YEAR/ ITEM #	DESCRIPTION	ORIGINAL PRICE	CODE
1977			
7518-1	Invisible Danger	1	C
7518-2	Edge of Adventure	1	C
7518-3	Emergency Rescue	1	C
7518-4	Path of Danger	1	C

EQUIPMENT SETS

YEAR/ ITEM #	DESCRIPTION	ORIGINAL PRICE	CODE
1977			
7528-1	Aqua Laser	2.40	C
7528-2	Treacherous Dive	2.40	C
7528-3	Fusion Bazooka	2.40	C
7538-1	Magna Tools	3.60	C
7538-2	Helipack	3.60	C
7538-3	Sonic Scanner	3.60	C

VEHICLE/PLAYSETS

YEAR/ ITEM #	DESCRIPTION	ORIGINAL PRICE	CODE
1977			
7570	Rocket Command Center	10.99	B
7571	Rocket Command Center Super Adventure Set Including Gor	14.59	B
8000	Super Joe Equipment case	3.95	F

ROLE PLAY

YEAR/ ITEM #	DESCRIPTION	ORIGINAL PRICE	CODE
	Laser Communicator	2.75	B

SERIES 1 1982

FIGURE SETS

ITEM #	NAME	DESCRIPTION	ORIGINAL PRICE	CODE
GI JOE				
6401	Stalker	Ranger	1.99	C
6402	Short Fuse	Mortar Soldier	1.99	C
6403	Breaker	Communications Officer	1.99	C
6404	Snake Eyes	Commando	1.99	C
6405	Zap	Bazooka Soldier	1.99	C
6406	Flash	Laser Rifle Trooper	1.99	C
6407	Scarlett	Counter Intelligence	1.99	C
6408	Rock'n Roll	Machine Gunner	1.99	C
6409	Grunt	Infantry Trooper	1.99	C
COBRA				
6423	Cobra	Infantry Soldier	1.99	C
6424	Cobra Officer	Infantry Officer	1.99	C
Mail Order (plus 5 flag-points)	Cobra Commander	Commanding Leader	1.75	BG
Mail Order (plus 5 flag-points)	Major Bludd	Mercenary	1.75	BG

VEHICLE SETS

ITEM #	NAME	DESCRIPTION	ORIGINAL PRICE	CODE
GI JOE				
6000	M.O.B.A.T.	Motorized Battle Tank with Steeler (driver)	14.99	B
6050	V.A.M.P.	Multi-Purpose Attack Vehicle with Clutch (driver)	5.99	B
6073	R.A.M.	Rapid Fire Motorcycle	2.99	B
COBRA				
	C.A.T.	Motorized Crimson Attack Tank	7.99	B

EQUIPMENT SETS

ITEM #	NAME	DESCRIPTION	ORIGINAL PRICE	CODE
GI JOE				
6052	H.A.L.	Heavy Artillery Laser with Grand Slam (operator)	5.99	B
6054	M.M.S.	Mobile Missile System with Hawk (operator)	5.99	B
6071	J.U.M.P.	Jet Pack with Platform	2.99	B
6075	F.L.A.K.	Attack Cannon	2.99	B

SERIES 2 1983

***Indicates a reissued or redesigned item**

FIGURE SETS

ITEM #	NAME	DESCRIPTION	ORIGINAL PRICE	CODE
GI JOE				
6401	Stalker*	Ranger	2.25	C
6402	Short Fuse*	Mortar Soldier	2.25	C
6403	Breaker*	Communications Officer	2.25	C
6404	Snake Eyes*	Commando	2.25	C
6405	Zap*	Bazooka Soldier	2.25	C
6406	Flash*	Laser Rifle Trooper	2.25	C
6407	Scarlett*	Counter Intelligence	2.25	C
6408	Rock'n Roll*	Machine Gunner	2.25	C
6409	Grunt*	Infantry Trooper	2.25	C
6410	Tripwire	Mine Detector	2.25	C
6411	Airborne	Helicopter Assault Trooper	2.25	C
6412	Snow Job	Arctic Trooper	2.25	C
6413	Torpedo	Navy S.E.A.L.	2.25	C
6414	Gung-Ho	Marine	2.25	C
6415	Doc	Medic	2.25	C
Mail Order Free with three Flag Points	Duke	Master Sergeant		BG
COBRA				
6423	Cobra*	Infantry Soldier	2.25	C
6424	Cobra Officer*	Infantry Officer	2.25	C
6425	Cobra Commander*	Commanding Leader	2.25	C
6426	Major Bludd	Mercenary	2.25	C
6427	Destro	Enemy Weapons Supplier	2.25	C

VEHICLE SETS

ITEM #	NAME	DESCRIPTION	ORIGINAL PRICE	CODE
GI JOE				
4025	Dragon Fly XH-1	Assault Copter with Wild Bill (pilot)	8.99	B
6010	Sky Striker XP-14F	F-14 Jet and Parachute with Ace (pilot)	14.95	B
6048	Wolverine	Armored Missile Vehicle with Cover Girl (driver)	6.39	B
6072	Polar Battle Bear	Sky Mobile	3.19	B
6093	A.P.C.	Amphibious Personnel Carrier	8.99	B
Asst. 6097	Falcon	Attack Glider with Grunt (pilot)	4.20	B
COBRA				
6051	H.I.S.S.	High Speed Sentry Tank with H.I.S.S. (driver)	6.39	B
6077	F.A.N.G.	Fully Armed Negator Gyro Copter	3.19	B
Asst. 6097	Cobra Glider	Attack Glider with Viper Pilot*	4.20	B

EQUIPMENT SETS

ITEM #	NAME	DESCRIPTION	ORIGINAL PRICE	CODE
GI JOE				
6065	Jump	Jet Pack and Platform with Grand Slam* (driver)	4.20	B
6074	Whirlwind	Twin Battle Gun	3.19	B
6088	Battle Gear Access. pk. #1	Pack of Figure Weapons & Accessories	1.59	B
Asst. 6086-1	Pac/Rats Flamethrower	Remote Control Weapon	1.59	B
Asst. 6086-2	Pac/Rats Machine Gun	Remote Control Weapon	1.59	B
Asst. 6086-3	Pac/Rats Missile Launcher	Remote Control Weapon	1.59	B
COBRA				
6083	S.N.A.K.E.	One-Man Battle Armor	1.75	B
GI JOE/COBRA				
6091	Pocket Patrol Pack	Display Case for 3 Figures with Belt Loop	3.60	B
6095	Collector Display Case	Display Case for 12 Figures and Bio Cards	3.82	B

PLAYSETS

ITEM #	NAME	DESCRIPTION	ORIGINAL PRICE	CODE
GI JOE				
6020	Headquarters Command Center	Headquarters Playset with Accessories.	24.99	B
COBRA				
6200 Sears	Headquarters Missile-Command Center	Headquarters Playset with Cobra Officer Cobra Soldier and Cobra Commander	34.99	B

SERIES 3 1983 - 1984

FIGURE SETS

ITEM #	NAME	DESCRIPTION	ORIGINAL PRICE	CODE
GI JOE				
6416	Mutt	Dog Handler with Dog (Junkyard)	2.25	C
6417	Spirit	Tracker with Eagle (Freedom)	2.25	C
6418	Rip-Cord	H.A.L.O. Jumper	2.25	C
6419	Road Block	Heavy Machine Gunner	2.25	C
6420	Recondo	Jungle Trooper	2.25	C
6421	Blow Torch	Flamethrower	2.25	C
6422	Duke	First Sergeant	2.25	C
COBRA				
6428	Baroness	Intelligence Officer	2.25	C
6429	Storm Shadow	Ninja	2.25	C
6431	Scrap Iron	Anti-Armor Specialist	2.25	C
6432	Fire Fly	Saboteur	2.25	C
Mail Order	Cobra Commander	Enemy Leader with Hood	2.25	BG

VEHICLE SETS

ITEM #	NAME	DESCRIPTION	ORIGINAL PRICE	CODE
GI JOE				
6005	Killer W.H.A.L.E.	Armored Hovercraft with Cutter (driver)	17.99	B
6049	S.H.A.R.C.	Submersible High-Speed Attack & Recon Craft with Deep Six (driver)	6.49	B

ITEM #	NAME	DESCRIPTION	ORIGINAL PRICE	CODE
Asst. 6055	Vamp Mark II*	Desert Jeep with *Clutch (driver)	6.49	B
6056	Slugger	Self-Propelled Cannon with Thunder (operator)	6.49	B
6079	Sky Hawk	V.T.O.L. Jet	3.29	B
6680 Sears	Vamp Jeep with H.A.L.	Attack Vehicle with Heavy Artillery Laser Cannon	6.49	B
COBRA				
6027	Rattler	Ground Attack Jet with Wild Weasel (pilot)	9.90	B
Asst. 6055	Stinger*	Night Attack Jeep with *Cobra Officer (driver)	6.49	B
6058	Water Moccasin	Swamp Boat with Copperhead (operator)	6.49	B
6064	Swamp Skier	Chameleon Vehicle with Zartan (operator)	4.20	B

EQUIPMENT SETS

ITEM #	NAME	DESCRIPTION	ORIGINAL PRICE	CODE
GI JOE				
Asst. 6129-1 Asst. 6129-2 Asst. 6129-3	Missile Defense Unit* Machine Gun Defense Unit* Mortar Defense Unit*	Battlefield Assortment: Mini Playsets with Accessories	2.29 ea.	B
Asst. 6125-1 Asst. 6125-2 Asst. 6125-3	Bivouac* Watchtower* Mountain Howitzer*	Battle Station Assortment: Mini-Playsets with Accessories	2.29 ea.	B
6092	Battle Gear Accessory Pack #2	Pack of Figure Weapons and Equipment	1.59	C
Mail Order 1 Flag Point	Manta	Marine Assault Nautical Air Driven Transport	1.25	B
Mail Order 1 Flag Point	Parachute	Parachute Pack with Working Parachute	1.50	B
COBRA				
6070	A.S.P.	Assault System Pod	3.29	B
Asst. 6081-1	C.L.A.W.*	Cobra Covert Light Aerial Weapons	1.80	B
6081-2	S.N.A.K.E.*	One-Man Armored Suit	1.80	B

VEHICLES

ITEM #	NAME	DESCRIPTION	ORIGINAL PRICE	CODE
GI JOE				
74450	RAM, HAL & VAMP (3-Piece Set)	Die Cast Metal GI Joe Vehicle/Equipment Sets	7.99	B
7444-1	Attack Vehicle (VAMP)	(same as above)	2.59	C
7444-2	Heavy Artillery Laser (HAL)	(same as above)	2.59	C
7444-3	Attack Cannon (FLAK)	(same as above)	2.59	C
7444-4	Battle Tank (MOBAT)	(same as above)	2.59	C
7444-5	Mobile Missile System (MMS)	(same as above)	2.59	C
7444-6	Rapid-Fire Motorcycle (RAM)	(same as above)	2.59	C

ROLE PLAY
(Life-sized Sets For Children)

ITEM #	NAME	DESCRIPTION	ORIGINAL PRICE	CODE
70309	Streamlined Goggles	GI Joe Swimwear	4.50	C / BG
74500	Swim Mask	GI Joe Swimwear	6	C / BG
74501	Swim Snorkel	GI Joe Swimwear	4.75	C / BG
74502	Swim Fins	GI Joe Swimwear	7.50	C / BG
74505	Swim Mask and Snorkel Set	GI Joe Swimwear	10.99	C / BG

SERIES 4
1984

FIGURE SETS

ITEM #	NAME	DESCRIPTION	ORIGINAL PRICE	CODE
GI JOE				
6436	Flint	Warrant Officer	2.29	C
6437	Snake Eyes*	Commando and Wolf (Timber)	2.29	C
6438	Bazooka	Missile Specialist	2.29	C
6439	Air Tight	Hostile Environment Trooper	2.29	C
6440	Lady Jaye	Covert Operations Officer	2.29	C
6441	Quick Kick	Silent Weapons Martial Artist	2.29	C
6442	Dusty	Desert Trooper	2.29	C
6443	Alpine	Mountain Trooper	2.29	C
6444	Footloose	Infantry Trooper	2.29	C
6445	Barbecue	Fire Fighter	2.29	C
6446	Shipwreck	Sailor and Parrot (Polly)	2.29	C
Asst. 6102/6108	Tripwire*	Mine Detector with Listen'n Fun Cassette Pack	3.75	C
COBRA				
Asst. 6063	Tomax	Crimson Guard Commander with Xamot (Opposite Twin)	4.49	C
6433	Buzzer	Mercenary (Dreadnok)	2.29	C
6434	Ripper	Mercenary (Dreadnok)	2.29	C
6435	Torch	Mercenary (Dreadnok)	2.29	C
6447	Tele-Viper	Communications Trooper	2.29	C
6448	Eel	Frogman	2.29	C
6449	Snow Serpent	Polar Assault Trooper	2.29	C
6450	Crimson Guard	Elite Trooper	2.29	C

VEHICLE SETS

ITEM #	NAME	DESCRIPTION	ORIGINAL PRICE	CODE
GI JOE				
6001	U.S.S. Flagg	Aircraft Carrier with Keel-Haul (Admiral)	89.99	B
6015	Mauler	Motorized Tank with Heavy Metal (driver)	16.99	B
6023	Bridge Layer	Bridge Laying Tank with Toll Booth (driver)	9.59	B
6053	A.W.E. Striker	All-Weather Environment Jeep with Crankcase (driver)	6.59	B
6057	Snowcat	Snow Half-Track Vehicle with Frost-Bite (driver)	6.59	B
6076	Silver Mirage	Motorcycle with Sidecar	3.29	B
6078	Armadillo	One-Man Mini-Tank	3.29	B
COBRA				
6024	Moray	Hydrofoil with Lamprey (pilot)	13.99	B
6069	Ferret	All-Terrain Vehicle	3.29	B
6686 Sears	Sentry and Missile System*	SMS Set with H.I.S.S. Tank	6.25	B
6687 Sears	Motorized Crimson Attack Tank	MOBAT Motorized Tank with New Colors*	12	B

EQUIPMENT SETS

ITEM #	NAME	DESCRIPTION	ORIGINAL PRICE	CODE
GI JOE				
Asst. 6085-1	Weapon Transport*	Battlefield Mini-Vehicles Assortment	2.29	B
Asst. 6085-2	Bomb Disposal*		2.29	B
Asst. 6129-1	Ammo Dump*	Battlefield Assortment	2.39	B
Asst. 6129-2	Forward Observer*	(same as above)	2.39	B
Asst. 6125-1	Check Point*	(same as above)	2.39	B
Asst. 6125-2	Air Defense*	(same as above)	2.39	B
6092	Battle Gear Accessory Pack #3	Pack of Figure Weapons and Equipment	2.39	C
COBRA				
Asst. 6081	Flight Pod*	One-Man Bubble Pod	2.39	B
Asst. 6085	Night Landing*	Mini Battlefield Vehicles Assortment	2.39	B
Asst. 6125	Cobra Bunker*	Battle station Assortment	2.39	B
Asst. 6129	Rifle Range*	Battlefield Accessory Assortment	2.39	B

PLAYSETS

ITEM #	NAME	DESCRIPTION	ORIGINAL PRICE	CODE
GI JOE				
6021	Tactical Battle Platform	Platform Playset	11.99	B

SERIES 5
1985

FIGURE SETS

ITEM #	NAME	DESCRIPTION	ORIGINAL PRICE	CODE
GI JOE				
6458	Leather Neck	Marine Gunner	2.35	C
6459	Low-Light	Night Spotter	2.35	C
6462	Main Frame	Computer Specialist	2.35	C
6463	Beach Head	Ranger	2.35	C
6465	Life Line	Rescue Trooper	2.35	C
6466	Ice Berg	Snow Trooper	2.35	C
6467	Road Block*	Heavy Machine Gunner	2.35	C
6468	Hawk*	Commander	2.35	C
6469	Sci-Fi	Laser Trooper	2.35	C
6470	Wet-Suit	Navy S.E.A.L.	2.35	C
6471	Dial Tone	Communications Expert	2.35	C
Mail Order	Sgt. Slaughter	Drill Instructor	3	BG
6691 Toys "R" Us	Special Mission: Brazil Claymore Dial-Tone* Wet-Suit* Leather-Neck* Main-Frame*	(Five-Figure Set with Video Cassette Tape) Covert Operations Communications Navy S.E.A.L. Marine Gunner Computer Specialist	11.75	B
COBRA				
6456	B.A.T.	Battle Android Trooper	2.35	C
6457	Zandar	Zartan's Brother Mercenary (Dreadnok)	2.35	C
6460	Monkey Wrench	Mercenary (Dreadnok)	2.35	C
6461	Dr. Mindbender	Master of Mind Control	2.35	C
6472	Zarana	Zartan's Sister Mercenary (Dreadnok)	2.35	C
6472	Zarana	(w/earrings) 2nd issue	2.35	C
6473	Viper	Infantry Trooper	2.35	C

VEHICLE SETS

ITEM #	NAME	DESCRIPTION	ORIGINAL PRICE	CODE
GI JOE				
6022	Tomahawk	Troop Transit Helicopter with Lift-Ticket (pilot)	12.99	B

ITEM #	NAME	DESCRIPTION	ORIGINAL PRICE	CODE
6030	H.A.V.O.C.	Heavy Artillery Vehicle Ordanance Carrier with Cross-Country (driver)	8.99	B
6031	Conquest X-30	Super-Sonic Jet with Slip Stream (pilot)	9.99	B
6061	Triple "T"	One-Man Tank with *Sgt. Slaughter (driver)	6.69	B
6066	Devil Fish	High-Speed Attack Boat	3.39	B
6067	L.V.C. Recon Sled	Low-Crawl Vehicle Cycle	3.39	B
COBRA				
6014	Night Raven S-3P	Surveillance Jet with Drone Pod and Strato Viper (pilot)	16.99	B
6041	Stun	Split Attack Vehicle with Motor-Viper (driver)	6.69	B
6042	Thunder Machine	Compilation Vehicle of Spare Parts with Thrasher (Dreadnok) driver	6.69	B
6062	Air Chariot	Vehicle with Serpentor "Cobra Emporer" (driver)	4.20	B
6068	Swamp Fire	Air/Swamp Transforming Vehicle with Color-Change (Dreadnok)	4.99	B
Sears	Air Assault	Air Vehicle (Dreadnok)*	4.99	B
Sears	Ground Assault	Land Vehicle (Dreadnok)*	4.99	B

EQUIPMENT SETS

ITEM #	NAME	DESCRIPTION	ORIGINAL PRICE	CODE
GI JOE				
Asst. 6130		Outpost Defender Mini Playset with Accessories*	2.39	B
COBRA				
Asst. 6130	*Surveillance Port	Mini Playset with Accessories	2.39	B
Asst. 6096	Battle Gear Accessory Pack #4	Package of Figure Equipment	2.39	B
COBRA				
Asst. 6099-1	Jet Pack*	One-Man Jet Set	1.89	B
Asst. 6099-2	Hydro Sled*	Mini-Vehicle with Access.	1.89	B

PLAYSETS

ITEM #	NAME	DESCRIPTION	ORIGINAL PRICE	CODE
6003	Terror Drome	Armored Headquarters with Firebat Jet and A.V.A.C. (pilot)	44.99	B

SETS FOR CHILDREN

ITEM #	NAME	DESCRIPTION	ORIGINAL PRICE	CODE
3000	Paint-A-Figurine	Figure and Paint Set	4.59	B
3575	Color-Vue Pencil By Number	Drawing Set with New Colors	2.95	B
8138	Listen'n Play	Book/Cassette Set	6.99	B

SERIES 6 1986-1987

FIGURE SETS

ITEM #	NAME	DESCRIPTION	ORIGINAL PRICE	CODE
GI JOE				
6153	Sgt. Slaughter's	(Three-Figure Set)	7.30	C
Toys "R" Us	Renegades			
	Red Dog	Renegade Commando		
	Taurus	Renegade Commando		
	Mercer	Renegade Commando		
6475	Crazy Legs	Air Assault Trooper	2.43	C
6476	Falcon	Green Beret	2.43	C
6477	Psych-Out	Deceptive Warfare Trooper	2.43	C
6478	Law & Order	M.P. with Dog (Order)	2.43	C
6480	Jinx	Ninja Intelligence Fighter	2.43	C
6481	Tunnel Rat	Underground Explosive Expert	2.43	C
6482	Chuckles	Undercover M.P.	2.43	C
6483	Outback	Survivalist	2.43	C
6486	Gung-Ho*	Marine in Dress Blues	2.43	C
6488	Fast Draw	Mobile Missile Specialist	2.43	C
6491	Sneak Peek	Advanced Recon Trooper	2.43	C
Mail Order 5 Flag Points	The Fridge	Physical Training Instructor		BG
Mail Order	Steel Brigade Trooper	(Buyer could select his own name, patch, specialty and file card)	7.50	BG
COBRA				
6154	Cobra-La Team	(Three-Figure Set)	7.30	C
Toys "R" Us	Golobulus	Cobra-La Leader		
	Nemesis Enforcer	Cobra-La Trooper		
	Royal Guard	Cobra-La Guard		
6474	Cobra Commander*	Cobra Leader with Battle Armor	2.43	C
6479	Crystal Ball	Hypnotist	2.43	C
6484	Big Boa	Troop Trainer	2.43	C
6485	Raptor	Falconer	2.43	C
6487	Crocmaster	Reptile Trainer	2.43	C
6490	Techno-Viper	Battlefield Technician	2.43	C

VEHICLE SETS

ITEM #	NAME	DESCRIPTION	ORIGINAL PRICE	CODE
GI JOE				
6002	Defiant Space Shuttle Complex	Space Shuttle, Space Station, Crawler Vehicle with Payload (Shuttle Astronaut) and Hard Top (Crawler driver)	99.99	B
6004-1	Crossfire-Alfa	Radio Control Vehicle with Rumbler (driver)	54.99	B
6004-2	Crossfire-Delta	(same as above)	54.99	B
6038	Persuader	Laser Tank with Back-Stop (driver)	6.89	B
Asst. 6087-1	Road Toad	Tow Vehicle with accessories	2.39	B
Asst. 6087-2	Coastal Defender	Mini-Vehicle with Access.	2.39	B
COBRA				
6026	Mamba	Attack Copter with Two Removable Pods with Gyro-Viper (pilot)	9.50	B
6029	Maggot	3-in-1 Tank Vehicle with W.O.R.M.S. Driver	9.29	B
6039	Wolf	Arctic Terrain Vehicle with Ice Viper (driver)	6.89	B
6040	Sea Ray	Combination Submarine/Jet with Sea Slug (Pilot)	6.89	B
6070	Dreadnok Air Skiff	Mini-Set with Zanzibar (pirate leader)	4.29	B
Asst. 6087-3	Buzz Boar	Underground Attack Vehicle	2.39	B
6170	Pogo	Ballistic Battle Ball	3.49	B
6171	Dreadnok Cycle	Compilation Cycle with Gunner Station	3.49	B

EQUIPMENT SETS

ITEM #	NAME	DESCRIPTION	ORIGINAL PRICE	CODE
6098	Vehicle Gear Accessory Pack #1	Vehicle Weapon and Accessory Pack	2.39	B
Asst. 6133-1	Antiaircraft Gun*	Motorized Action Packs	1.99	B
Asst. 6133-2	Helicopter Pack*	(same as above)	1.99	B
Asst. 6133-3	Radar Station*	(same as above)	1.99	B
Asst. 6133-4	Rope Walker*	(same as above)	1.99	B
6172	S.L.A.M.	Strategic Long-Range Artillery Machine	3.49	B
6677	Battle Gear Accessory Pack #5	Figure Accessory Pack	1.69	C
COBRA				
Asst. 6133-5	Rope Crosser*	Motorized Action Packs	1.99	B
Asst. 6133-6	Earth Borer *	(same as above)	1.99	B
Asst. 6133-7	Mountain Climber*	(same as above)	1.99	B
Asst. 6133-8	Pom-Pom Gun Pack*	(same as above)	1.99	B
GI JOE/COBRA				
6965	Battle Figure Collectors' Case	Carrying Case with Storage for 30 Figures	9.99	B

PLAYSETS

ITEM #	NAME	DESCRIPTION	ORIGINAL PRICE	CODE
GI JOE				
6006	Mobile Command Center	Three-Level Playset/Vehicle with Steam Roller (operator)	34.99	B

SERIES 7 1988

FIGURE SETS

ITEM #	NAME	DESCRIPTION	ORIGINAL PRICE	CODE
GI JOE				
6505	Blizzard	Arctic Attack Soldier	2.55	C
6507	Storm Shadow*	Ninja	2.55	C
6508	Repeater	Steadi-Cam Machine Gunner	2.55	C
6509	Shockwave	S.W.A.T. Specialist	2.55	C
6510	Charbroil	Flamethrower	2.55	C
6511	Hit & Run	Light Infantry Man	2.55	C
6512	Light Foot	Explosives Expert	2.55	C
6513	Hardball	Multi-Shot Grenadier	2.55	C
6514	Spearhead	Point Man with Bobcat (Max)	2.55	C
6516	Muskrat	Swamp Fighter	2.55	C
6517	Budo	Samurai Warrior	2.55	C
6253	Starduster	Special Pilot	4.50	BG
Mail Order 2 Flag Points		with Pocket Patrol Figure Carrying Case		
Target	Hit & Run*	Lt. Infantryman with Working Airborne Assault Parachute & Pack	4.75	C
GI JOE BATTLEFORCE 2000				
6522	Avalanche	Dominator Snow Tank driver	2.43	C
6522	Blaster	Vindicator driver	2.43	C
6523	Maverick	Vector Jet Pilot	2.43	C
6523	Blocker	Eliminator Driver	2.43	C
6524	Dodger	Marauder Motorcycle Driver	2.43	C
6524	Knockdown	Sky Sweeper Driver	2.43	C
6522-6696	Two-Figure Pack	Avalanche and Blaster	4.50	C
6523-6696	Two-Figure Pack	Maverick and Blocker	4.50	C
6524-6696	Two-Figure Pack	Dodger and Knockdown	4.50	C
GI JOE TIGER FORCE				
Asst. 6697-1	Duke*	First Sergeant/Squad Leader	2.55	C

ITEM #	NAME	DESCRIPTION	ORIGINAL PRICE	CODE
Asst. 6697-2	Roadblock*	Heavy Machine Gunner	2.55	C
Asst. 6697-3	Dusty*	Desert Trooper	2.55	C
Asst. 6697-4	Flint*	First Warrant Officer	2.55	C
Asst. 6697-5	Bazooka*	Missile Specialist	2.55	C
Asst. 6697-6	Tripwire*	Mine Detector	2.55	C
Asst. 6697-7	Lifeline*	Rescue Trooper	2.55	C
GI JOE NIGHT FORCE				
6709-1 Toys "R" Us	Two-Figure Pack	Lt. Falcon (Green Beret) with Sneak Peek (Advanced Recon)*	4.98	C
6709-2 Toys "R" Us	Two-Figure Pack	Outback (Survivalist) with Crazy-Legs (Assault Trooper)*	4.98	C
6709-3 Toys "R" Us	Two-Figure Pack	Psych-Out (Deceptive Warfare Specialist) with Tunnel Rat (Underground Explosive Expert)*	4.98	C
6710-1 Toys "R" Us	Two-Figure Pack	Repeater (Steadi-Cam Machine Gunner) with Charbroil (Flamethrower)*	4.98	C
6710-2 Toys "R" Us	Two-Figure Pack	Shockwave (S.W.A.T. Specialist) with Light Foot (Explosives Expert)*	4.98	C
6710-3 Toys "R" Us	Two-Figure Pack	Spearhead (Point Man) with Bobcat (Max) and Muskrat (Swamp Fighter)*	4.98	C
GI JOE/COBRA				
6282 Target	Ultimate Enemies	Special two-Figure Pack with Muskrat *(Swamp Fighter) and Voltar* (Destro's General)	4.19	C
COBRA				
6506	Iron Grenadier	Destro's Elite Trooper	2.55	C
6513	Toxo-Viper	Hostile Environment Trooper	2.55	C
6515	Astro-Viper	Cobranaut Space Trooper	2.55	C
6519	Hydro-Viper	Underwater Assault Trooper with Manta Ray	2.55	C
6520	Voltar	General with Condor (Bird)	2.55	C
6521	Road Pig	Biker/Mercenary (Dreadnok)	2.55	C
6523	Super Trooper	Metal/Plastic Jet Pack	1.00	B
Mail Order Two Flag Points		Trooper with Carry Case		

VEHICLE SETS

ITEM #	NAME	DESCRIPTION	ORIGINAL PRICE	CODE
GI JOE				
6012	Rolling Thunder	Armored Missile Launcher Tank with Armadillo (driver)	22.99	B
6016	Phantom X-19	Stealth Fighter Jet with Ghost Rider (pilot)	18.99	B
6028	Mean Dog	3-in-1 Armored Vehicle with Wild Card (driver)	10.49	B
6032	Warthog	Armored Infantry Fighting Vehicle with Sgt. Slaughter* (driver)	9.29	B
6045	Skystorm	X-Wing Chopper with Windmill (pilot)	7.99	B
Asst. 6135-1	Tank Car	Motorized Vehicle Pack	1.99	B
Asst. 6135-2	Scuba Pack	Motorized Vehicle Pack	1.99	B
Asst. 6135-3	A.T.V.	Motorized Vehicle Pack	1.99	B
6161	Swamp Masher	Nine-Wheeled Swamp Vehicle	3.99	B
6253	Desert Fox	Six-Wheeled Desert Jeep with Skidmark (driver)	5.99	B
6285	R.P.D.	Remote Piloted Vehicle	2.89	B
6388	Locust	Attack Copter/Bomber	6.99	B
GI JOE BATTLEFORCE 2000				
6643	Marauder	Futuristic Motorcycle/Tank	6.49	B
6644	Sky Sweeper	Antiaircraft Tank	6.49	B
6645	Vindicator	Futuristic Hovercraft	6.49	B
6646	Dominator	Futuristic Snow Tank	6.49	B
6647	Eliminator	Futuristic Armored Jeep	6.49	B
6648	Vector Jet	Future Jet with Gun Pod	6.49	B
GI JOE TIGER FORCE				
6669	Tiger Paw	A.T.V. Tracked Vehicle	3.99	B
6670	Tiger Shark	Attack Speed Boat	5.99	B
6671	Tiger Cat	Armored Half-Track with Frost Bite (pilot)*	7.99	B
6672	Tiger Fly	Attack Helicopter with Recondo (pilot)*	11.99	B
6673	Tiger Rat	Attack Anti-Armored Plane with Skystriker (pilot)	12.99	B
NIGHT FORCE (GI JOE) Toys "R" Us				
6704	Night Storm*	3-in-1 Tank Vehicle	8.75	B
6705	Night Blaster*	Laser Tank	5.75	B
6706	Night Raider*	Armored Tank Vehicle	5.49	B
6707	Night Shade*	Jet/Sub Attack Vehicle	5.49	B
6708	Night Striker*	Armored Hovercraft*	20.99	B
6709	Night Scrambler	Amphibious Personnel Carrier	9.99	B
COBRA				
6018	B.U.G.G.	Amphibious Command Vehicle with Secto-Viper (driver)	15.99	B
6033	D.E.M.O.N.	Dual Elevating Multi-Ordnance Neutralizer with Ferret (driver) (Iron Grenadiers)	10.49	B

ITEM #	NAME	DESCRIPTION	ORIGINAL PRICE	CODE
6059	Despoiler	Vehicle with Destro* (Iron Grenadiers Leader)	4.49	B
6252	Stellar Stilletto	Trans-Orbital Fighter Craft with Star-Viper (pilot)	6.29	B
6254	Fang II	V.T.O.L. Plane	6.29	B
6649	A.G.P.	Anti-Gravity Pod with Nullifier (Iron Grenadiers pilot)	5.99	B
Asst. 6135-1	Gyro Copter*	Motorized Vehicle Packs	1.99	B
Asst. 6135-2	Rocket Sled*	Motorized Vehicle Packs	1.99	B
Asst. 6135-3	Scuba Pack*	Motorized Vehicle Packs	1.99	B

EQUIPMENT SETS

ITEM #	NAME	DESCRIPTION	ORIGINAL PRICE	CODE
GI JOE				
Asst. 6133-1	Mine Sweeper*	Motorized Action Packs	1.99	B
Asst. 6133-2	Mortar Launcher*	Motorized Action Packs	1.99	B
Asst. 6133-3	Double Machine Gun*	Motorized Action Packs	1.99	B
COBRA				
Asst. 6133-4	Dreadnok Battle Ax*	Motorized Action Packs	1.99	B
Asst. 6133-5	Twin Missile Launcher*	Motorized Action Packs	1.99	B
Asst. 6133-6	Machine Gun Nest*	Motorized Action Packs	1.99	B
6165	IMP	Armored Rocket Launcher	3.99	B
6191	Cobra Battle Gear Accessory Pack #6	Figure Accessory Pack	2.99	B
6287	Adder	Missile Launcher	2.99	B
6299	Battle Barge	Armored Floating Gunner Station	2.10	B

PLAYSETS

ITEM #	NAME	DESCRIPTION	ORIGINAL PRICE	CODE
GI JOE BATTLEFORCE 2000				
Sears	Future Fortress	Six Battleforce Vehicles into One Headquarters	34.99	B

SERIES 8
1988-1989

FIGURE SETS

ITEM #	NAME	DESCRIPTION	ORIGINAL PRICE	CODE
GI JOE				
6525	Recoil	Long-Range Recon Trooper	2.55	C
6526	Scoop	Video Technician Trooper	2.55	C
6527	Count Down	Astronaut	2.55	C
6528	Snake Eyes*	Commando	2.55	C
6532	Rock'n Roll*	Machine Gunner	2.55	C
6533	Stalker*	Tundra Rangar	2.55	C
6543	Back Blast	Antiaircraft Gunner	2.55	C
6544	Downtown	Mortar Trooper	2.55	C
6545	Deep-Six*	Deep-Sea Diver	2.55	C
GI JOE SLAUGHTER'S MARAUDERS				
Asst. 6560-1	Sgt. Slaughter*	Division Sergeant	2.55	C
Asst. 6560-2	Mutt & Junkyard*	K-9 Officer & Dog	2.55	C
Asst. 6560-3	Low-Light*	Night Trooper	2.55	C
Asst. 6560-4	Spirit*	Tracker with Freedom (Eagle)	2.55	C
Asst. 6560-5	Barbecue*	Fire-Fighter	2.55	C
Asst. 6560-6	Footloose*	Infantry Soldier	2.55	C
GI JOE BATTLEFORCE 2000				
6531	Dee-Jay	Laser Trooper	2.55	C
COBRA				
6529	Alley-Viper	Urban-Assault Trooper	2.55	B
6530	T.A.R.G.A.T.	Trans-Orbital Assault Trooper	2.55	B
6534	H.E.A.T.-Viper	Flamethrower	2.55	B
6535	Gnawgahyde	Poacher with Boar (Dreadnok)	2.55	B
6546	Frag-Viper	Grenade Thrower	2.55	B
6547	Night-Viper	Night Trooper	2.55	B
6548	Annihilator	Aerial Trooper	2.55	B
COBRA PYTHON PATROL				
Asst. 6623-1	Officer*	Patrol Officer	2.55	C
Asst. 6623-2	Viper*	Patrol Leader	2.55	C
Asst. 6623-3	Tele-Viper*	Communications Officer	2.55	C
Asst. 6623-4	Crimson Guard*	Patrol Guard	2.55	C
Asst. 6623-5	Copperhead*	Patrol Pilot	2.55	C
Asst. 6623-6	Trooper*	Patrol Infantry	2.55	C

VEHICLE SETS

ITEM #	NAME	DESCRIPTION	ORIGINAL PRICE	CODE
6220	Crusader with Avenger*	Space Shuttle with Scout Craft and Pay-Load (Pilot)	24.99	B
6231	Thunder Clap	3 in 1 Cannon Transport with Long Range (Driver)	22.99	B
6240	Raider	2 in 1 Battle Tank with Hot-Seat (Driver)	13.99	B
6254	Arctic Blast	Thundra Assault Vehicle with Wind Chill (Driver)	6.29	B
6255	Mudfighter	Low-Flying Bomber with Dog Fight (Pilot)	6.29	B
6638	Tri-Blaster	One-Man Auto Pilot Vehicle	2.59	B
6639	Radar Rat	One-Man Auto Pilot Vehicle	2.59	B

ITEM #	NAME	DESCRIPTION	ORIGINAL PRICE	CODE
GI JOE TIGER FORCE				
6674	Tiger Fish*	Reoutfitted Power Boat	4.29	B
6675	Tiger Sting*	Reoutfitted Attack Jeep	6.29	B
GI JOE SLAUGHTER'S MARAUDERS				
6717	Armadillo*	One-Man Rocket Tank	4.29	B
6718	Lynx*	Cannon Tank	6.29	B
6719	Equalizer*	Armored Rocket Launcher Tank	14.99	B
GI JOE BATTLE FORCE 2000				
6286	Pulverizer	Laser Tank with Extendable Gun	4.19	B
GI JOE NIGHT FORCE				
Toys "R" Us	Night Ray Night Boomer Night Scrambler	3 Vehicle Set	29.99	B
GI JOE/COBRA				
6852	Mudfighter* and Cobra H.I.S.S. II*	Benny's Two-Vehicle/Four-Figure Set Mudfighter with Dog-Fight* and Cobra H.I.S.S. with Track-Viper* and Two Bonus figures (randomly selected)	34.99	B
COBRA				
6222	Condor Z-25	2-in-1 Jet Fighter Bomber with Aero-Viper (driver)	20.49	B
6242	Razor Back	Destro's Dual Elevating Armored Tank Vehicle with Wild Boar (Destro's driver)	10.49	B
6246	H.I.S.S. II	Troop Transport Tank with Track-Viper (driver)	8.39	B
6271	Evader	Vehicle with Darklon (Destro's Arms Commander)	4.49	B
6633	Devastator	One-Man Auto-Pilot Vehicle	2.59	B
6637	Hovercraft	One-Man Auto-Pilot Vehicle	2.59	B
PYTHON PATROL (COBRA)				
6618	Asp*	Re-outfitted Gun Emplacement	4.29	B
6619	Stun*	Re-outfitted Split-Attack Vehicle	8.39	B
6620	Conquest*	Re-outfitted Fighter Jet	13.59	B
6633	Devastator	One-Man Auto-Pilot Vehicle	2.59	B
6637	Hovercraft	One-Man Auto-Pilot Vehicle	2.59	B
COBRA PYTHON PATROL				
6618	Asp*	Re-outfitted Gun Emplacement	4.29	B
6619	Stun*	Re-outfitted Split-Attack Vehicle	8.39	B
6620	Conquest*	Re-outfitted Fighter Jet	13.59	B

SERIES 9
1990

FIGURE SETS

ITEM #	NAME	DESCRIPTION	ORIGINAL PRICE	CODE
GI JOE				
6561	Capt. Grid-Iron	Combat Leader	2.55	C
6563	Topside	Navy Trooper	2.55	C
6565	Sub-Zero	Arctic Mortar Trooper	2.55	C
6566	Ambush	Camouflage Trooper	2.55	C
6567	Salvo	Rocket Launcher Specialist	2.55	C
6568	Free-Fall	Paratrooper	2.55	C
6574	Rampart	Shore Patrol	2.55	C
6575	Stretcher	Medic	2.55	C
6576	Bullhorn	Crisis Intervention Specialist	2.55	C
6577	Pathfinder	Jungle Trooper	2.55	C
GI JOE SKY PATROL				
Asst. 6200-1	Altitude	Air Assault Trooper with parachute	2.55	C
Asst. 6200-2	Airborne	Air Assault Trooper with parachute	2.55	C
Asst. 6200-3	Drop Zone	Air Assault Trooper with parachute	2.55	C
Asst. 6200-4	Static Line	Air Assault Trooper with parachute	2.55	C
Asst. 6200-5	Skydive	Air Assault Trooper with parachute	2.55	C
Asst. 6200-6	Airwave	Air Assault Trooper with parachute	2.55	C
COBRA				
6137	Undertow	Scuba Diver (Iron Grenadiers)	2.55	C
6562	Night-Creeper	Ninja	2.55	C
6564	Rock Viper	Mountain Trooper	2.55	C
6569	Laser Viper	Laser Trooper	2.55	C
6570	S.A.W. Viper	Semi-Automatic Weapons Trooper	2.55	C
6571	Metal-Head	Anti-Tank Specialist	2.55	C
6573	Range Viper	Wilderness Trooper	2.55	C

VEHICLE SETS

ITEM #	NAME	DESCRIPTION	ORIGINAL PRICE	CODE
GI JOE				
6335	Retaliator	Bomber Copter with Claw and Updraft (driver)	6.99	B
6339	Avalanche	Snow Tank with Cold Front (driver)	6.99	B
6357	Hammerhead	Fast Attack Jeep	6.99	B
6372	Mobile Battle Bunker	Armored Bunker Tank	6.99	B
GI JOE SKY PATROL				
6110	Sky Havoc*	Armored Crawler with Skiff	6.99	B
6116	Sky S.H.A.R.C.*	Flying Sub	6.99	B
6118	Sky Raven*	Jet Bomber	6.99	B
6361	Sky Hawk*	V.T.O.L. Copter	6.99	B
COBRA				
6112	Rage	Urban Assault Tank	6.99	B
6320	Hammerhead	Amphibious Tank with Multi-Vehicles and Decimator (driver)	6.99	B
6343	Hurricane	V.T.O.L. Jet with Vapor (driver)	6.99	B
6369	Dominator	Tank into Helicopter (Iron Grenadiers)	6.99	B
6380	Dictator	Dual Action Vehicle with Overlord (Cobra Governor)	6.99	B
6385	Piranah	Fast Attack Boat	4.60	B

PLAYSETS

ITEM #	NAME	DESCRIPTION	ORIGINAL PRICE	CODE
GI JOE				
6320	General	Mobile Headquarters and Launch Platform with Locust Copter and Major Storm (driver)	44.99	B

SERIES 10
1991

FIGURE SETS

ITEM #	NAME	DESCRIPTION	ORIGINAL PRICE	CODE
GI JOE SONIC FIGHTERS				
6311	Tunnel-Rat*	Underground Commando	4.99	C
6312	Law*	M.P. (Military Police Officer)	4.99	C
6313	Dial-Tone*	Communications Specialist	4.99	C
6314	Dodger*	Vehicle Expert	4.99	C
GI JOE				
6580	Dusty*	Desert Trooper with Coyote (Sandstorm)	2.60	C
6581	Low-Light*	Night Fighter	2.60	C
6582	Big-Ben*	S.A.S. Trooper	2.60	C
6583	General Hawk*	Commander with Flight Pack	2.60	C
6586	Heavy-Duty	Anti-Armored Trooper	2.60	C
6587	Sci-Fi*	Laser Trooper	2.60	C
6588	Red-Star	Oktober Guard Officer	2.60	C
6591	Grunt*	Infantry	2.60	C
6592	Snake-Eyes*	Commando	2.60	C
6593	Tracker	Wilderness Specialist with Inflatable Raft	2.60	C
6594	Mercer*	Ex-Cobra Officer	2.60	C
GI JOE SUPER SONIC FIGHTERS				
6597	Lt. Falcon*	Green Beret	5.29	C
6598	Zap*	Ground Artillery Soldier	5.29	C
6631	Rock'n Roll*	Machine Gunner	5.29	C
6632	Psych-Out*	Psychological Warfare Specialist	5.29	C
GI JOE ECO WARRIORS				
6815	Flint*	Eco-Leader	3.99	C
6816	Clean-Sweep	Chemical Expert	3.99	C
6817	Ozone	Atmosphere Expert	3.99	C
GI JOE HALL OF FAME				
6019 Target	Duke*	12-inch Master Sergeant with Lights and Sound Weapons (First 12-inch GI Joe since 1976)	14.99	B
COBRA SONIC FIGHTERS				
6316	Lampreys*	Amphibious Assault Trooper	4.99	C
6351	Viper*	Infantry	4.99	C
COBRA				
6584	Crimson Guard* Immortal	Elite Guard	2.60	C
6585	Snow Serpent*	Snow Trooper	2.60	C
6586	Desert Scorpion	Desert Specialist with Giant Scorpion	2.60	C
6588	Red Star	Oktober Guard	2.60	C
6590	Incinerator	Flamethrower	2.60	C
6595	B.A.T.*	Battle Android Trooper	2.60	C
6596	Cobra Commander*	Commander	2.60	C

ITEM #	NAME	DESCRIPTION	ORIGINAL PRICE	CODE
Toys "R" Us	Rapid-Fire	Fast Attack Expert with "Revenge of the Pharoahs" Video Cassette	4.60	C

COBRA
SUPER SONIC FIGHTERS

6599	Major Bludd*	Mercenary	5.29	C
6630	Road Pig*	Biker (Dreadnok)	5.29	C

COBRA
ECO WARRIORS

6818	Cess-Pool	Eco-Leader	3.99	C
6819-1	Toxo-Viper	Hostile Environmental Trooper	3.99	C
6819-2	Toxo-Viper II*	Maintenance Antarb Trooper	3.99	C
6820	Sludge-Viper	Chemical Trooper	3.99	C

VEHICLE SETS

GI JOE

6215	Badger	Fast Attack Jeep	4.49	B
6226	Attack Cruiser	AntiAircraft Launcher	6.99	B
6321	Brawler	Rocket Launcher Tank	12.99	B
6326	Battle Copter	Copter Vehicle with Major Altitude (pilot)	5.99	B
6344	Battle Wagon	4 X 4 Attack Truck	24.99	B
6811	Skymate	Glider with Skymate (Air Commando Trooper)	5.99	B
6812	Cloudburst	Glider with Cloudburst (Air Commando Trooper)	5.99	B
6737	Spirit*	Glider with Tracker (Air Commando Trooper)	5.99	B

COBRA

6217	Paralyzer	Fast-Attack Tank	4.49	B
6221	Ice Sabre	Ice Vehicle	7.99	B
6325	Interrogator	Battle Copter with Interrogator (copter pilot)	5.99	B
6813	Sky Creeper	Glider with Air Commando Leader (Sky Creeper)	5.99	B
6814	Night Vulture	Glider with Air Commando Infantry (Night Vulture)	5.99	B

COBRA
ECO-WARRIORS

6144	Septic Tank	Eco-Tank	7.99	B

ROLE-PLAY (Life-Sized Sets for Children)

GI JOE

6035	Duke	Electronic Battle Gear Set with Helmet, Goggles and Electronic Gun	13.99	B

SERIES 11
1992

FIGURE SETS

ITEM #	NAME	DESCRIPTION	ORIGINAL PRICE	CODE
GI JOE				
6725	Duke	Master Sergeant	2.65	C
6726	Wet-Suit*	Navy Seal	2.65	C
6727	Road Block*	Master Gunner	2.65	C
6728	Big Bear	Russian Bazooka Trooper (Oktober Guard)	2.65	C
6739	General Flagg	Second Commander	2.65	C
6740	Gung-Ho*	Marine	2.65	C
6741	Barricade	Bunker Buster Specialist	2.65	C
6742	Wild Bill*	Cavalry Officer	2.65	C
6751	General Hawk*	Talking Commander	5.99	C
6752	Stalker*	Talking Ranger	5.99	C
Mail Order	Steel Brigade*	Special Figure In New Colors (Green, Blue and Gold)	8.95	BG

GI JOE
ECO-WARRIORS

6821	Deep-Six*	Marine Bio-Trooper and Finback (Dolphin)	3.99	C
6822	Barbecue*	Fire Trooper	3.99	C

GI JOE
NINJA FORCE

6731	Storm shadow*	Ninja Force Commander	2.65	C
6732	Dojo	Ninja Swordsman	2.65	C
6733	Nunchuk	Nunchuk Ninja	2.65	C
6734	T'Jbang	Bola Ninja	2.65	C

GI JOE
DRUG ELIMINATION FORCE

6745	Bullet-Proof	Federal Marshall	3.99	C
6746	Mutt*	Canine Officer with Dog (Junkyard)	3.99	C
6747	Cutter*	Coast Guard	3.99	C
6748	Shockwave*	S.W.A.T. Officer	3.99	C
6749	Headman	Drug Lord (Evil Headhunters)	3.99	C
6750	Head Hunter	Elite Guard (Evil Headhunters)	3.99	C

GI JOE
HALL OF FAME

6826	Duke*	12-inch Master Sergeant with Lights and Sound Weapons (2nd Version)	19.99	B
6828	Snake-Eyes*	12-inch Commando with Lights and Sound Weapons	19.99	B
6829	Stalker*	12-inch Ranger with Lights and Sound Weapons	19.99	B

COBRA

6729	Destro*	Arms Dealer	2.65	C
6730	Flak-Viper	Anti Aircraft Soldier	2.65	C
6743	Firefly*	Saboteur	2.65	C
6744	Eel*	Scuba Diver	2.65	C
6753	Cobra Commander*	Talking Cobra Leader	5.99	C
6754	Overkill	Talking B.A.T. Leader	5.99	C

COBRA
NINJA FORCE

6735	Slice	Ninja Swordsman	2.65	C
6736	Dice	Ninja Commando	2.65	C
Mail Order	Ninja-Viper*	(Same mold as 1984 Storm Shadow)	3.75	BG

COBRA
HALL OF FAME

6827	Cobra Commander*	12-inch Cobra Leader with Lights and Sound Weapons	19.99	B

VEHICLE SETS

GI JOE

6227	Barracuda	One-Man Diving Sub	4.69	B
6232	Patriot	Mortar Launcher Crawler	6.99	B
6241	Fort America	Bombed-Out Fort into Tank	16.99	B
6262	Sonic Desert Apache	Desert Helicopter	16.99	B
6755	Storm Eagle	Water-Shooting Jet	8.99	B
6824	Ace*	Battle Copter with Lead Pilot (Ace)	5.99	B

GI JOE
ECO WARRIORS

6145	Eco-Striker*	Water-Shooting A.T. Buggy	5.99	B

COBRA

6228	Rat	One-Man Hovercraft	4.69	B
6234	Parasite	Armored Personnel Carrier	6.99	B
6238	Air Devil	Aerialist Glider with Air Devil	5.99	B
6239	Earthquake	Construction Loader	12.99	B
6756	Heli-Viper	Battle Copter with Heli-Viper (Infantry Pilot)	5.99	B

COBRA
ECO WARRIORS

6823	Toxo-Zombie	Battle Copter with Lead Pilot (Toxo-Zombie)	5.99	B

PLAYSETS

GI JOE

6249	Headquarters*	Command Center with Electronic Lights and Sound	39.99	B

COBRA
ECO WARRIORS

6146	Toxo-Lab	Toxic Laboratory	8.99	B

GI JOE/COBRA

	Collectors' Case	For Battle Figures	9.99	B

ROLE PLAY (Life-sized Sets for Children)

GI JOE

6245	Snake-Eyes Battle Gear	Dress-Up and Weapons Set	13.99	B
	GI Joe	Headband and Wristband Set	7.99	B
	"Stars and Stripes Forever"	Wall Posters	3.99	Poster
	"To the Rescue"	Wall Posters		
2535	Trace Plates	Pencil & Crayon Tracer Sets	6.50	B

HALL OF FAME SERIES
1993

FIGURE SETS

ITEM #	NAME	DESCRIPTION	ORIGINAL PRICE	CODE
GI JOE				
6111	Grunt	12-inch Infantry Squad Leader with Weapon	12.99	B
6114	Heavy Duty	12-inch Heavy Ordinance Specialist with Weapon	12.99	B
6117	Battle Command Duke	12-inch Talking Master Sergeant with Spring Action Weapon	34.99	B
6127	Flint	12-inch Warrant Officer with Spring Action Weapon	18.99	B
6128	Rock'n Roll	12-inch Machine Gunner with Spring Action Weapon	18.99	B
6837	Ace	12-inch Jet Pilot with Spring Action Weapon	18.99	B

ITEM #	NAME	DESCRIPTION	ORIGINAL PRICE	CODE
6848	Storm Shadow	12-inch Ninja with Spring Action Weapon	18.99	B
6849	Gung-Ho	12-inch Dress Marine with Spring Action Weapon	18.99	B
COBRA				
6839	Destro	12-inch Enemy Weapons / Supplier with Spring Action Weapon	18.99	B
6924	Rapid-Fire	Toys "R" Us edition		

VEHICLE SETS

ITEM #	NAME	DESCRIPTION	ORIGINAL PRICE	CODE
GI JOE				
6119	Rhino	24-inch General Purpose All-Terrain Vehicle	34.99	B

UNIFORM/EQUIPMENT SETS

ITEM #	NAME	DESCRIPTION	ORIGINAL PRICE	CODE
GI JOE				
27500-1	Arctic Assault	Polar Mission Gear with Spring Action Weapons	8.99	C
27500-2	Underwater Attack	Underwater Mission Gear with Spring Action Weapons	8.99	C
27500-3	S.W.A.T. Assault	Undercover Mission Gear with Spring Action Weapons	8.99	C
27500-4	Light Infantry	Combat Mission Gear with Spring Action Weapons	8.99	C

BATTLE CORPS SERIES 1993

ITEM #	NAME	DESCRIPTION	ORIGINAL PRICE	CODE
GI JOE FIGURES				
6169	Bulletproof	Urban Commander	2.99	C
6229	Mutt & Junkyard	K-9 Officer & Attack Dog	2.99	C
6757	Law	Military Police	2.99	C
6758	Mace	Undercover Operative	2.99	C
6759	Muskrat	Heavy Fire Specialist	2.99	C
6761	Long Arm	First Strike Specialist	2.99	C
6763	Roadblock	Heavy Machine Gunner	2.99	C
6764	Wet Suit	Navy SEAL	2.99	C
6767	Gung-Ho	U.S. Marine	2.99	C
6768	Barricade	Bunker Buster	2.99	C
6771	Duke	Battle Commander	2.99	C
6772	Frostbite	Arctic Commander	2.99	C
6773	Keel-Haul	Admiral	2.99	C
6774	Backblast	Anti-aircraft Soldier	2.99	C
6777	Colonel Courage	Strategic Commander	2.99	C
6778	Leatherneck	Infantry/Training Specialist	2.99	C
6779	Snowstorm	High-tech Snow Trooper	2.99	C
6780	Outback	Survival Specialist	2.99	C
6794	Wild Bill	Aero-scout	2.99	C
6798	General Flagg	GI Joe General	2.99	C
6861	Bazooka	Missile Specialist	2.99	C
6862	Cross-Country	Transport Expert	2.99	C
6863	Ice Berg	Arctic Assault Trooper	2.99	C
6864	Beach-Head	Ranger	2.99	C
no#	Flint		2.99	C
no#	Shipwreck		2.99	C
no#	Dialtone		2.99	C
no#	Metal-Head		2.99	C
no#	Beach-Head		2.99	C
no#	Viper		2.99	C
COBRA FIGURES				
6168	Headhunter Stormtrooper	Elite Urban Crime Guard	2.99	C
6186	Headhunter	Cobra Street Fighter	2.99	C
6762	Gristle	Urban Crime Commander	2.99	C
6766	Flak-Viper	Anti-Aircraft	2.99	C
6769	Firefly	Cobra Saboteur	2.99	C
6775	Crimson Guard Commander	Cobra Elite Officer	2.99	C
6776	Cobra Commander	Cobra Supreme Leader	2.99	C
6781	Night Creeper Leader Cobra	Ninja Supreme Leader	2.99	C
6782	Dr. Mindbender	Master of Mind Control	2.99	C
6799	Cobra Eel	Underwater Demolitions	2.99	C
no#	Alley-Viper		2.99	C

BATTLE CORPS VEHICLES (WITH FIGURES) 1993

ITEM #	NAME	ORIGINAL PRICE	CODE
GI JOE			
6867	Shark with Cutter	19.99	B
6868	GI Joe Ghost Striker X16-Jet with Ace	39.99	B
COBRA			
6162	Cobra Detonator with Nitro-Viper	32.99	B
no#	Scorpion (with Manta Ray vehicle)	9.99	B

STREET FIGHTER II SERIES 1993

ITEM #	NAME	ORIGINAL PRICE	CODE
GI JOE FIGURES			
81081	Guile	3.99	C
81082	Chun-Li	3.99	C
81083	Blanka	3.99	C
81084	M. Bison	3.99	C
81085	Ken Masters	3.99	C
81086	Ryu	3.99	C
81091	Edmond Honda	3.99	C
81092	Dhalsim	3.99	C
81093	Zangief	3.99	C
81094	Vega	3.99	C
81095	Balrog	3.99	C
81096	Sagat	3.99	C

STREET FIGHTER II VEHICLES (WITH FIGURES)

ITEM #	NAME	ORIGINAL PRICE	CODE
6201	Crimson Cruiser with M. Bison	8.99	B
6687	Beast Blaster with Blanka & Chun-Li	8.99	B
6790	Sonic Boom Tank with Guile	8.99	B

STREET FIGHTER II PLAYSETS (WITH FIGURES)

ITEM #	NAME	ORIGINAL PRICE	CODE
	Dragon Fortress with Ryu & Ken Masters	17.99	B

NINJA FORCE SERIES 1993

ITEM #	NAME	DESCRIPTION	ORIGINAL PRICE	CODE
GI JOE FIGURES				
6871	Snake Eyes	Covert Mission Specialist	2.99	C
6874	Scarlett	Counter Intelligence Specialist	2.99	C
6875	Banzai	Rising Sun/Ninja	2.99	C
6876	Bushido	Snow Ninja	2.99	C
COBRA FIGURES				
6796	Slice	Cobra Ninja Swordsman	2.99	C
6872	Zartan	Master of Disguise	2.99	C
6873	Cobra	Night Creeper Cobra Ninja	2.99	C

NINJA RAIDERS SERIES 1993

ITEM #	NAME	ORIGINAL PRICE	CODE
GI JOE FIGURES			
6792	T'Gin-Zu	3.25	C
COBRA FIGURES			
6793	Red Ninja	3.25	C

MEGA-MARINES SERIES 1993

ITEM #	NAME	DESCRIPTION	ORIGINAL PRICE	CODE
GI JOE FIGURES				
6927	Gung-Ho	Mega-Marines Commander	4.99	C
6928	Clutch	Monster Blaster	4.99	C
6931	Mirage	Bio-artillary Expert	4.99	C
6932	Blast-Off	Flame Thrower	4.99	C
COBRA FIGURES				
6929	Cobra Mega Viper	Mega Monster Trainer	4.99	C
6934	Cobra Cyber Viper	Cybernetic Officer	4.99	C

MEGA MONSTERS SERIES 1993

ITEM #	NAME	ORIGINAL PRICE	CODE
6071	Cobra Bio-Viper	5.99	C
6073	Cobra Monstro-Viper	5.99	C

STAR BRIGADE SERIES 1993

ITEM #	NAME	ORIGINAL PRICE	CODE
GI JOE FIGURES			
81101	Payload	3.25	C
81102	Countdown	3.25	C
81103	Ozone	3.25	C
81104	Roadblock	3.25	C
COBRA FIGURES			
81105	Cobra Astro-Viper	3.25	C
81106	Cobra TARGAT	3.25	C

ARMOR-TECH STAR BRIGADE SERIES 1993

ITEM #	NAME	ORIGINAL PRICE	CODE
ARMOR-TECH VEHICLES (WITH FIGURES)			
no#	Starfighter with Sci-Fi	34.95	B
no#	Armor-Bot with Hawk	34.95	B
GI JOE PLAYSETS (WITH FIGURES)			
no#	Ambush & Lowlight Wal-Mart special edition	29.99	B

HASBRO DIRECT (MAIL ORDER) PRODUCTS 1993

ITEM #	NAME	ORIGINAL PRICE	CODE
GI JOE			
no#	Deep-Six	3.75 + 1 flag point	B
no#	General Hawk	3.75 + 1 flag point	B
no#	Interrogator	3.75 + 1 flag point	B
no#	Major Altitude	3.75 + 1 flag point	B
no#	Fast Draw	3.75 + 1 flag point	B
no#	Repeater	3.75 + 1 flag point	B
no#	Shock Wave	3.75 + 1 flag point	B
no#	Bud	3.75 + 1 flag point	B
no#	Big Bear	3.75 + 1 flag point	B
no#	Big Ben	3.75 + 1 flag point	B
no#	Spirit	3.75 + 1 flag point	B
no#	Sub-Zero	3.75 + 1 flag point	B
no#	Dee-Jay	3.75 + 1 flag point	B
no#	Stalker	3.75 + 1 flag point	B
COBRA			
no#	Snow Serpent	3.75 + 1 flag point	B

BATTLE CORPS SERIES 1994

ITEM #	NAME	ORIGINAL PRICE	CODE
GI JOE FIGURES			
81005	Metal-Head	3.29	B
81002	Dialtone	3.29	B
81003	Shipwreck	3.29	B
81006	Viper	3.29	B
81088	Beach-Head	3.29	B
81008	Stalker	3.29	C
81007	Life-Line	3.29	C
81004	Ice-Cream Soldier	3.29	C
81097	Snow Storm	3.29	C
81001	Flint	3.29	C

ITEM #	NAME	DESCRIPTION	ORIGINAL PRICE	CODE
COBRA FIGURES				
81012	Major Bludd		3.29	C
81098	Night Creeper Leader		3.29	C
81089	Alley-Viper		3.29	C

SHADOW NINJA SERIES
1994

ITEM #	NAME	DESCRIPTION	ORIGINAL PRICE	CODE
GI JOE FIGURES				
81141	Snake-Eyes		4.99	C
81142	Storm Shadow		4.99	C
81147	Bushido		4.99	C
81144	Slice		4.99	C
81145	Nunchuck		4.99	C
COBRA FIGURES				
81146	Night Creeper		4.99	C

STAR BRIGADE SERIES
1994

ITEM #	NAME	DESCRIPTION	ORIGINAL PRICE	CODE
GI JOE FIGURES				
81052	Duke		3.29	C
81053	Sci-Fi		3.29	C
81055	Space Shot		3.29	C
81117	Payload		3.29	C
81118	Roadblock		3.29	C
81054	Effects		3.29	C
81058	Lobotomaxx		3.29	C
81059	Predacon		3.29	C
81061	Carcass		3.29	C
81119	Countdown		3.29	C
81127	Ozone		3.29	C
COBRA FIGURES				
81056	Cobra Commander		3.29	C
81057	Cobra Blackstar		3.29	C
6132	GI Joe Manta-Ray			
6134	Cobra Scorpion			
6139	GI Joe Razor-Blade			
6147	GI Joe Blockbuster w/Wind-Chill			

POWER FIGHTERS SERIES
1994

ITEM #	NAME	DESCRIPTION	ORIGINAL PRICE	CODE
GI JOE FIGURES				
81035	Gears		4.99	C
COBRA FIGURES				
81036	Techno-Viper		4.99	C

MANIMALS SERIES
1994

ITEM #	NAME	DESCRIPTION	ORIGINAL PRICE	CODE
GI JOE FIGURES				
81038	Warwolf		4.99	C
81039	Slythor		4.99	C
81041	Vortex		4.99	C
81042	Iguanus		4.99	C
81044	Zig-Zag		4.99	C
81043	Spasma		4.99	C

HALL OF FAME FIGURES & VEHICLES
1994

ITEM #	NAME	DESCRIPTION	ORIGINAL PRICE	CODE
6044	Combat Camo Duke			
6049	Combat Camo Roadblock			
6127	Battle Bazooka Flint			
6128	Gatlin' Blastin' Rock 'n Roll			
6159	Battle Pack Major Bludd			
6089	Karate Choppin' Snake-Eyes			
6791	Strike Cycle			

30th SALUTE SERIES
1994

ITEM #	NAME	DESCRIPTION	ORIGINAL PRICE	CODE
81045	Action Soldier			
81046	Action Pilot			
81047	Action Marine			
81048	Action Sailor			
6857	30th Salute Original Team Set			
81271	30th Salute Black Action Solder			
no#	Action Green Beret Promo Figure		5 proofs	
no#	12" Green Beret Promo Figure		20 proofs	

Epilogue

If you, as I, grew up in the 1960s, you probably remember it as one of the most exciting decades of the twentieth century. The United States propelled its space program from a brief, one-man Mercury flight, to the landing of an Apollo crew on the moon. Technology accelerated at dizzying speed toward our era of personal computers(at rummage sales!). Vietnam and the "flower power" generation collided head-on. And GI Joe was born.

Charging to the top of the toy market in 1964, GI Joe had defied all odds—succeeding as a boy's "doll" in an increasingly anti-military time. The new product line singlehandedly defined a new toy category: "action figure."

During the 60s and 70s, GI Joe basically was one personality. Since 1982, with the reintroduction of GI Joe as a 3¾ inch figure, Hasbro has produced over 300 different figures, portraying over 260 personalities.

The Real American Hero is recognized as one of the hottest-selling toys of our time. Year after year, he maintains leadership among toys, defending his top-ten position in the American toy market.

The enduring success of GI Joe makes him an eminently collectible item. GI Joe figures and accessories sometimes command thousands of dollars. This is, in part, because in a time when toy makers are competing to market collectible toys, only a few, such as GI Joe, enjoy the status of being a classic, established name. As often as GI Joe changes, he remains the same.

Bibliography

Comic Books
GI Joe, ©Ziff-Davis Publishing Company, New York, New York

GI Joe, ©Marvel Comics Group, Inc., New York, New York, and ©DC Comics, New York, New York

Photography & Prop Styling
Vincent Santelmo/The Official Action Figure Warehouse, Rego Park, New York
Sunny Fine/Sunshine Productions, New York, New York

Resources
Some of the information in this book was obtained from the following periodicals:

Sales Marketing Management Magazine, New York: "The Story of GI Joe—Old Taboo, New Market" (1965).

New York Times Magazine, New York: "Failing War Toy Succeeds as Peaceful Adventurer" (1970); "Dolls at War" (1970).

National Review, New York: "What Have They Done to GI Joe?" (1970).

Businessweek, New York: "A Toy-Maker Builds on a TV Name!" (1971).

Dayton Daily News, Dayton, Ohio: "Toying with Success" (1982).

Newsweek, New York: "GI Joe: Back in Action" (1982).

Spinning Wheel: "The Saga of GI Joe" (1983).

New Times, Phoenix, Ariz.: "Soldier of Fortune" (1988).

Chicago Tribune Magazine, Chicago: "No Ordinary Joe" (1989).

Hasbro, Inc., New York/Pawtucket:
"GI Joe Chronology: The Past 25 Years" (1989).
"GI Joe a Real American Hero, 1964-1989" (1989).
"The History of Hasbro" (1989).

Cross Advertising, Kenosha, Wisc.: "GI Joe Advertisements in 1960s Comic Books" (1990).

Sunday Journal Magazine, Providence: "Toy Soldiers: The Men Who Design Hasbro's Secret Weapons" (1991).

Star Telegraph, Fort Worth: "Playing for Keeps," and "GI Joe Stays on Top by Changing with the Times" (1992).

Collectible Toys and Values: "The Hasbro Interview."

Important Notice

The information in this book, including valuations, has been compiled from reliable reference sources. Every effort has been made to eliminate errors and questionable data. The publisher and the author will not be held responsible for losses which may occur in the purchase, sale or other transaction of items because of information contained herein.

The complete GI Joe product history, from the 1960s to the 1990s, including item number, item name, year of manufacture, original price, contents, etc., has been cataloged from the following references:

- GI Joe product literature
- Comics
- Yearbooks
- Hasbro sales catalogs
- Sears catalogs
- J.C. Penney catalogs
- Montgomery Ward catalogs
- Simpson Sears catalogs
- Hasbro product listings
- GI Joe items in the author's own collection.

About the Author

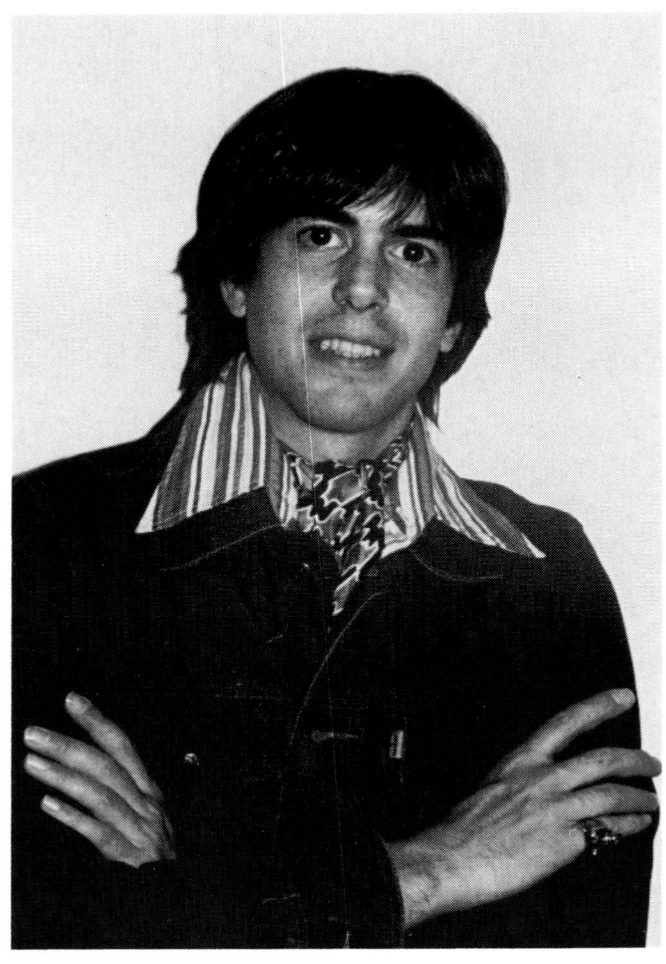

Described by the *Wall Street Journal* as the "world's foremost GI Joe collector," Vincent Santelmo grew up in the 1960s in the Bronx, New York. In early 1983, he discovered a 1960s GI Joe, still in its original box, at Chick Darrow's Fun Antiques, a toy store in New York City. "GI Joe was my favorite as a kid," Vincent says, "and after I was reunited with him, I decided to start collecting again. My mania for them has continued ever since!"

From the early '80s until today, Santelmo has built an impressive collection of original GI Joes. In 1989, for GI Joe's twenty-fifth anniversary, Santelmo appeared on New York's Channel 7, on WOR radio, and in newspapers such as the *Wall Street Journal*. Through the years he has published numerous articles about GI Joe in collector magazines.

Of his books, he comments, "Now I have written *The Complete Encyclopedia to GI Joe*, and *The Official 30th Anniversary Tribute to GI Joe*, in dedication to my fantastic, plastic friend who spent so much time with me when we were young."

Today, Santelmo is a comic book artist, photographer, and musician. He also writes and illustrates other definitive novels.